WE BUILD A CITY

POEMS AND GRAPHICS

KINGA TÓTH

Trans. By Sven Engelke and Kinga Tóth

KFS
Newton-le-Willows

Published in the United Kingdom in 2020
by The Knives Forks And Spoons Press,
51 Pipit Avenue,
Newton-le-Willows,
Merseyside,
WA12 9RG.

ISBN 978-1-912211-58-6

Acknowledgents:

First published by Parasitenpresse, Cologne, as *Wir Bauen Eine Stadt* (2019).

LOTTERY FUNDED

Supported using public funding by
ARTS COUNCIL ENGLAND

CONTENTS

WE BUILD A CITY
POEMS AND GRAPHICS

Micro Z-A-S

The hatted woman welded onto the box
in her womb a golden ball
projecting celestial bodies
on the cupola her hat a planetring
mirrors citylight
sirens bounce off it
in her shoulderneedles she collects
city traffic lights in her belly
a glassball penetrated
with metalscrew
from double ground up
bi-lensed ocular her leg hangs
from the mounting
in box diopterrollers
thimbles and demagnifiers
on the right hand spins
an a8 stand prepared for preparations
her womb is heatresistant
not molding into ironinjection
in telescopemirror of loupebody
liquid crystals darkle
reciprocally into the eyes
on tube mounting a lithiumglass
for sharpness control in borosilicate
weight of sinking
celestial bodies engraved
6.5cm is an injection and sunaxis
The lowest swivel is vertical
horizontal clockwise backwise
inside eggs sharpening the retinal instruments

with by mouth by metalspoon
drives into her femalescrew
she sends light slide to her hat
upper section of sending pipe
is welded to the cervical vertebra
sending facility opens the lower lens
above lies black coating of roof
dims from circular arc
falling planetoids out
on dome roof floats
oval solarsystem off
crank pushes spoon
into glassball
screw drives itself into roof
the last earth arrives

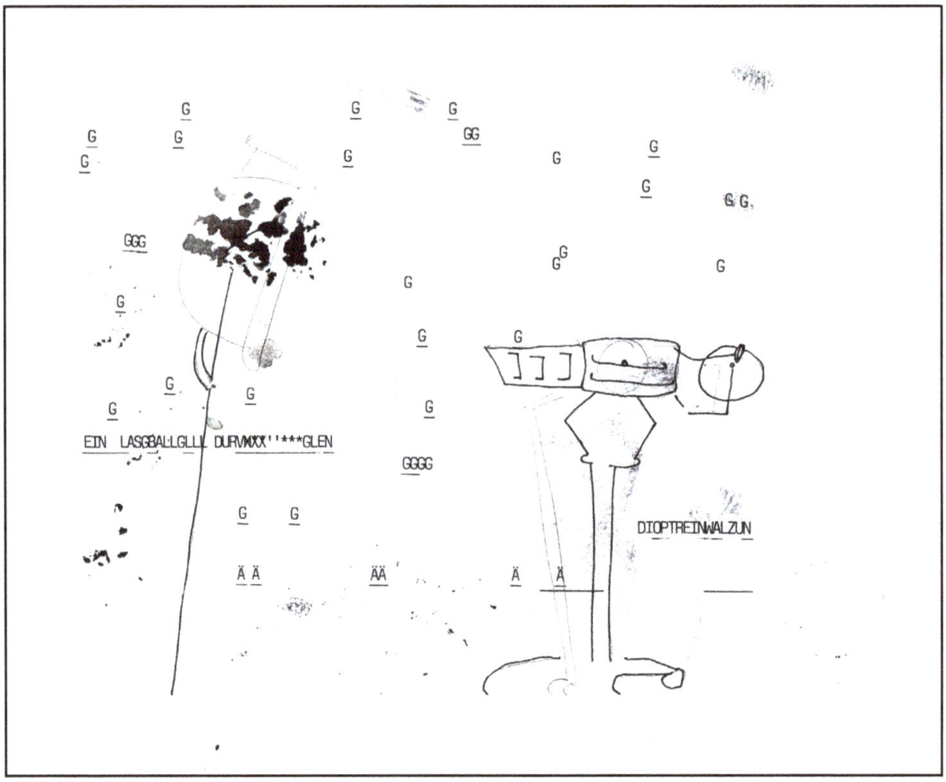

MAKER

<wie sie kommunizieren
wie sie programmieren
the mountains fall was
wird passieren am ende wie sie kleben>

rubberwalls on coordinates
singleparts on vectormountains
squashed white knödel
on their coordinatecluster
referencepoints are coatings
how to build miniobjects
of synthetic hair and buttons
rubberprints are the newbricks
in layers sand water modeling clay
rubbernumber stones on plan
numbers and notes are the scrapings
in sandgrids organs
moving coordinates inside collection
streaked plaits past programming

<wann ist die nächste krise
warum nennst du sie so>

all ordered in totemtowers
as flat right angle
red burgundy purple black
first grids
then coatings
until refinement here
no *lichthoflandschaft?*

<aber das system erlaubt es nicht
die berge zu bauen>

below
from black nodal point
changing units emerge
sometimes lines thrust together
sometimes afar
planned yellow flakes
straggle in trinity
buttons inside cluster
gain around at end yellow
knots sand what is their matter
and of white a compression
a dot construction inside graphicon
finally dense newpoints
newdeed inner contour

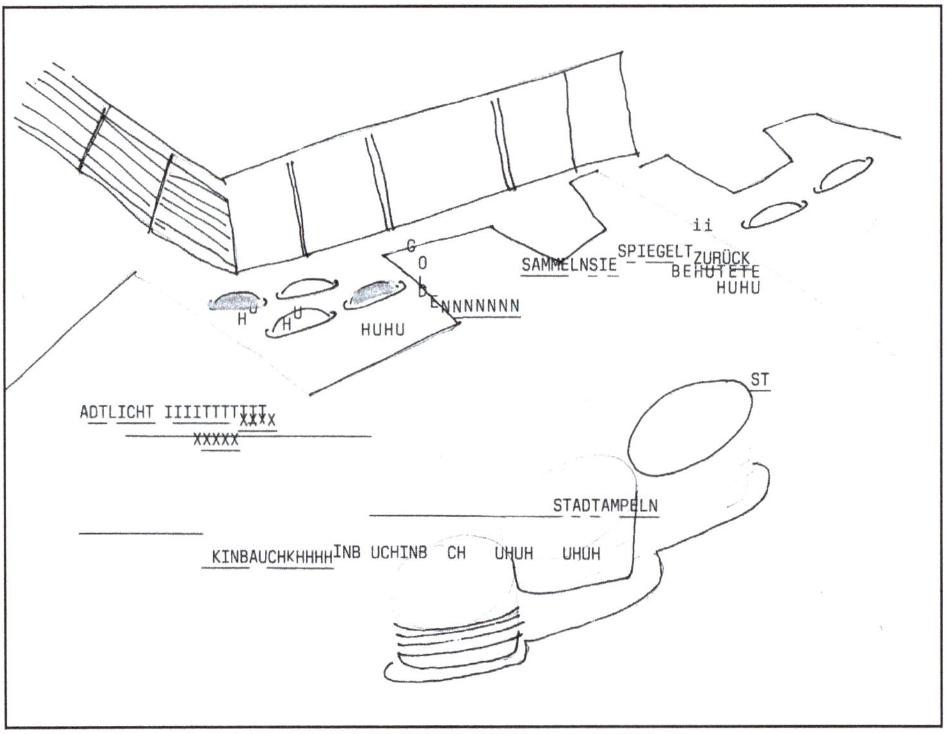

PARADISE

at first keyboard pray before
ogden rboden nice just two suffrages

place one's hair lacquer what hangs out
stairs are cleaned kneeling
in the flat (zero) heel to the station
only the sinners knock
at afternoon comes donation
their self-carved altar is brought
for the poor on the foldstool
room for three they don't open her the door
the children are taught rhymes
what will mary do to them if you
dip the index finger into the water
lower the roller blinds
so that the nonbelonging
see nothing while singing
can't paradise be different
where there is nothing but afternoon
where I don't have to point at me
three times with ashes sinner
where there is interval when
they want to mislead us
that's the signal not to care
while kneeling not until hard

and everything can go on the wall
these people are scary
stop watches measure the selftorment
there are special shops for tormentbelts

the saints are drudged for what
a diadem is folded out of their hair
and lacquered wounds are disinfected
the innocent don't knock

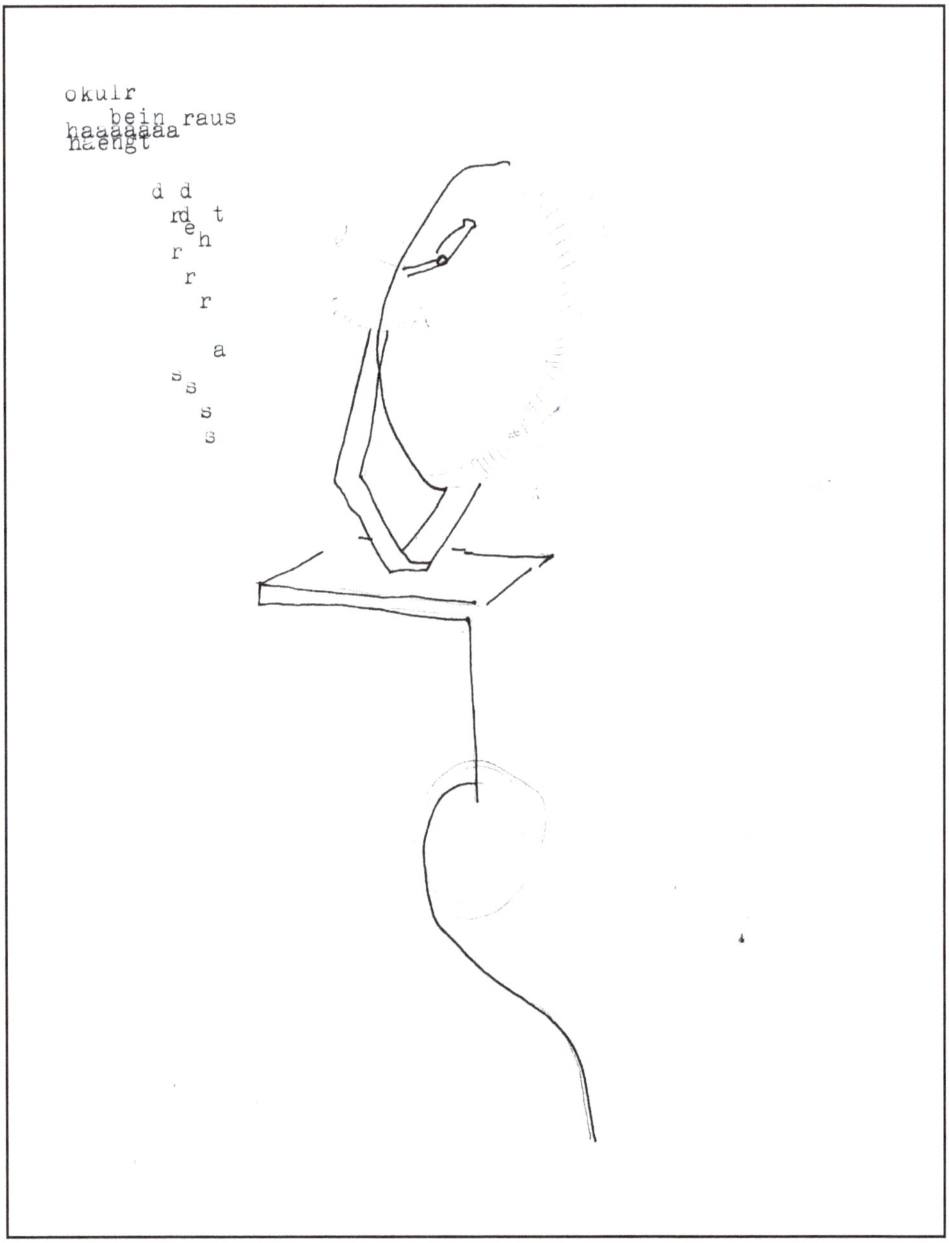

RETINA

to the film by Darko Dragicevic

in need
the children run
in dresses of the same color
drawn lines in their eyes
they enter another world
the weaver protects them
she composes music on the threads
puts on their thick socks
the cemeteries are also drawn
so they become birds
her footprint is horny

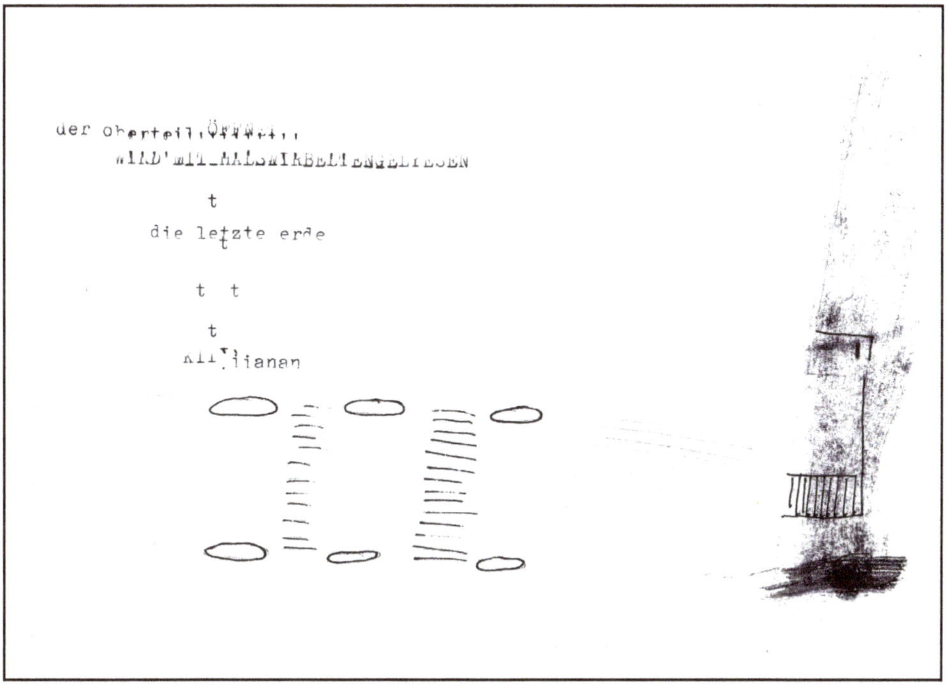

they try the spring bed
stick when

they are overgrown with threads
without it nothing is seen
the weaver's tear is soft on the screen
she inhales at the window sucks fishing line
can be pulled out of a hole
on the pullover
the sheepman protects her
then with whom who has strawberries
fine house on the chimney
the drawingsnails are running
into heaven

"WE BUILD A CITY"

(Palais Schaumburg)

for Kai Franz's Ploppermaschine

i.

sandmountains loadingfacility
with needlehead
deletes the tunnel
under the sticky bridges
marblecells
in plasma wakehouses
we build a city
first filling of the tunnel
its end in the ditch where
the pebbles where the railway
melt down in glue
the women in blue spots
in brows the earth
ferries built on them
the loadingfacility
loads them with triple code
the transition is knotty
and rough so that the passersby
do not sneak with vines
they hold on
to the upper layer
where children and construction workers
stroll attempt
jump the white
the radiant fragile
like in spiderfabric bind
the skyscrapers

ii.

they fasten the cement mixer
let adhesive river into the sand
no more fall the planning program
signs the colors with idnumbers
icerink blue email 3
filling ferries white quartz 18
portion transfer sand 20
on land 50 in the tunnels concrete
the needlehead prepares the vectors
the planer prepares the ironframework
of the city this city becomes semicircular
grate becomes the rule of the
machine functions in 4 strips of the
loadingfacility horizontal
road control and
the smelters on the vertical axis
grippers and cranes on the grate
mainrail and institutions
clean on the connective points
looking city at the end of the skull
lift the semisphere
make photocopies for citizens

iii.

gold clots from the old town
bones been relocated by grippers
bones of the old in the dirt
organic fabric flowing plastic
the partner city a totempole
made of five cells inside microchip

with populational geographical
data built on each other
their pattern the base of the semicircle
the citypeople talk to each other
with soundorgancodes 1.197 1.198
the spray gun gets closer and closer
in the city center at crossroads
double strikes the movement of
water with software regulated also
the colors purple pink blue and white
between them passages in institute
the porcelaincomponents mix
no fence on the tracks

iv.

the inhabitants of the vertical
partner city enter in colorful
halls football match in artificial hairlawn
between the cities with horn-shaped
antennas they communicate the results
to those who stayed at home those who
work on molecular webs
in the industrial districts
girls prepare the chemical substances
in their hair lilac jagged straps
can be cracked into the grill grid
then it is possible to enter the building site
on their breast tires of coal
of hydrogen of nitrogen
of calcium from phosphor 27
produced for hours
when the waterplanes fall on them
their skins remain soft

on their epithelial cells under limestone
gazing the gatewebs on their
strawvectors tendons and joints
on the connection points the history
vibrant subcutaneous tissue in specimens
exemplified in museums and schools
in the end no line again
on top of the net on the sky
color and code are liquid here
sprinkle the plopper automats
trickles the sandy glue

v.

pocket batteries
red cord blue cord
moves the nozzleheads
blows in eggtablets
the tillerhead now
separate the wax
and the colors
remove broken bits of building
on the bridges above
base glaze mirrors
the nightlamps
and bullglass lights
airplanes land

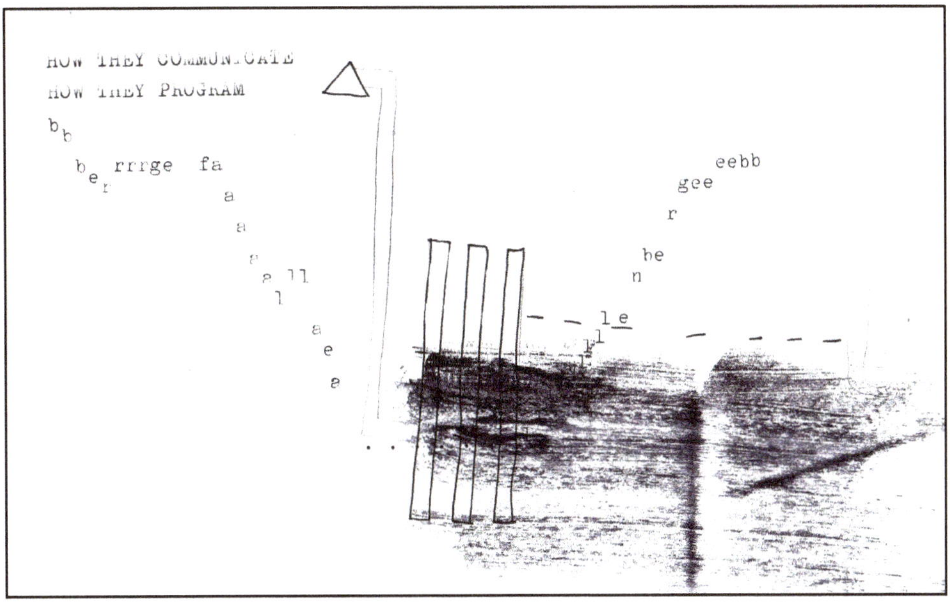
HOW THEY COMMUNICATE
HOW THEY PROGRAM

WHALE

in the Whalestomach 3d plastic buoys
are bound to the veins
on the enterofur the tube is
swung left
ttdd
mmrr
the two men are sitting
at two ends of the freezer
in front of them the female handlebar
with voicey saliva goes to the beginner
through to the other
the sticks are of different length
reach to the flutist at 1 o'clock
to the trumpeter in the afternoon
the saxophonist 10 o'clock
9 and 3 are the cooling instruments
back longer with two
the disciplined cembalo
straight back only arm movement
cracks of pressure as well as
the driller's xylophone in the chest
into the bubble this ball is
let in 7 o'clock
in dashboard seven main veins
lead to the exhaust of the whale
250 miles away on a barge
the other group orchestra
its rotation is contrary the inner
grabs the whale presses
stationary swinging in water

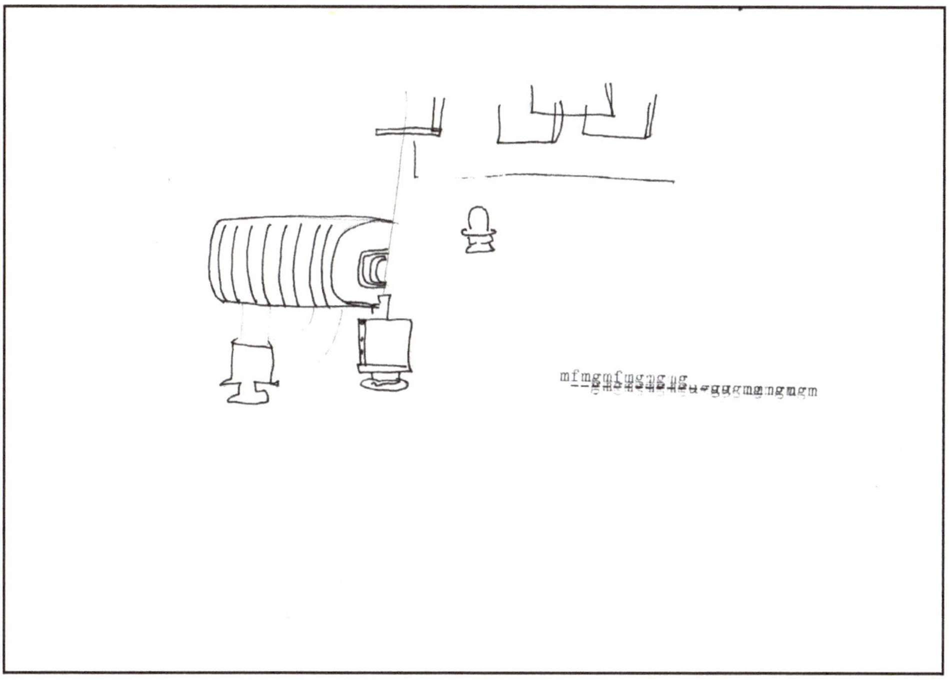

in whaleexhaust meet the inner
and the outer vibration
in hole 200 miles
ddttmmrrmmrrddtt
r r d d l t m m
the zoologist saves the signaling
on his recording device
in two waves on the bark
kindergarten groups are
shown the applause tempo
the kindergarten teacher shows
shrug shoulderbow out in
out in circle the children
draw the knapsack with shoulders
the whale eats algae
no fear inside the children
standing around the orchestra when
they know the turning already
observe the outer xylophonist
whose head nods

the end of the handlebarsticks
of clocks entangled 9 10 11 12 1 2 3
3-6
when the flutist changes the instrument
also the clocks in shouldercircles
the xylophone's jacket has shoulder pads
in rear rows the movement is
still visible they're mistaking
The message not 150
at 3 rows in circles
in growing order in
inner containtank get
opposite xylophones
table the whale becomes slower
the water flow supports
the coral island movement
the children's orchestra sees
a huge hump from the
bankdirection 100 on the
zoologists' spectrograph then it
rises in elliptical form
his pulsation coincides with the barkfacility
his traveldirection the bark 50
The water querls concentric
the outer circular rings of its
two centers intersect
the kindergarten teacher lets
hands fall amazed the children
lead the spinning forward
turn back the shoulderbelt
9 new sheets begins the xylophone
Grabs the sticks fall down
on the dock and
the membranewall
of the containtank
nothing gets hurt
this meeting is happening

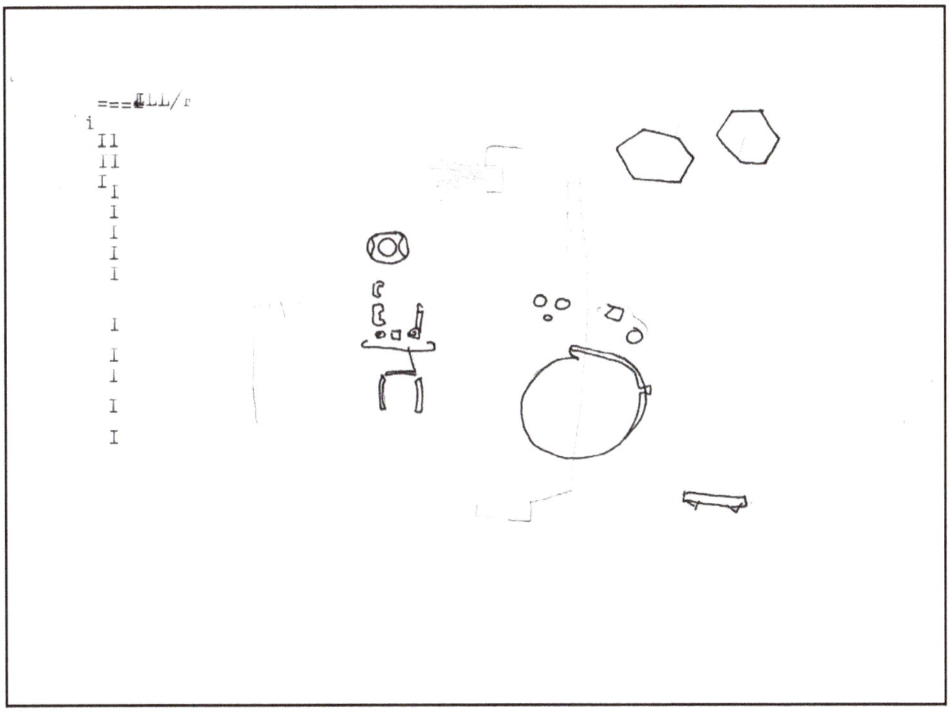

the whale sends his bubble
with diaphragmpressure that
crashes on the trampolines
inside of the orchestra
the writingsticks on the spectrograph
fold out and fly on the xylophone
here it fits on the rectangles don't
make mistakes in the contactkeeping
the cembalists arrival for 2 o'clock
the first waterwave waterstream
the next breath of the whale
his last drops fall towards 9 10-9
the kindergarten children gather
the crashes in sandbox buckets
The kindergarten teacher weighs quietly
ajar to the zoologistapparatus
in water in two stripes whale and woman
breathing saved the woman gets ready
and goes to the trampoline
jumps into the next tank at 10

the selected
7 kindergarten children give their buckets to
the orchestra and follow each separately
the kindergarten teacher new chapel
covered by containtanks 50
and remove the adults
and the finished orchestras
wave to the whale
with inflamed sticks
in whalememory this experience
and the smell of roasting handlebarsticks
is imprinted for 25 years the bark is
slowed by fluorescent buoys
and by neon poles the city
helps to store this experience 100
the zoologist determines
from those who stayed outside
the next seven children
of the containtank carry
fluorescent key-cases
the next arrival
with combination of new
visual and electronic
developments of the kindergarten teacher comes to be
makes telescopes from neoncylinders
the children take the positions 200
the zoologist builds the sticks from pointers
of the spectrograph in different lengths
according to the clocknumbers
on the outer and inner dials
on 7 mainpoints
the participants fasten
onto the network to the conductors
uncover the previous notation sheets
and draw newer signals
between the clusters at 250
mark the start line

wind the clock dials
the children's seats in the dial
crash opener

SUNALLEY

<full throttle life>

on napsétány vibrating flamingos
with broken legs no wcroof
the corner is not for ladies
jump in skirts between them
in shoppingwindow a burgundysofa one
should think all two are there
when they get jostled

i broke off his other leg
he says that it's a lightlabel
it's not at the window, but
at the backwall
and with his stretched leg
in a flamecut series connection
the glowbulbs hang on him
at the belly, where his wing
starts in leg there were two
the other there in lowerpart, he doesn't brood
because of the crack it's clear to see
he doesn't use what was left
swings on the belly
when he's seated on the sofa
this is how the strawberryshake got its name
they give him a straw
bend over broken flamingo and
uprightly they don't stick two
into the foam, by turns
suck under the lamp
pee into the package silently

the screamers finish also
when the new lamps
are carried outside
neonsign stands at the column
halfhuman pink wise
it is here on this corner
do not get lost

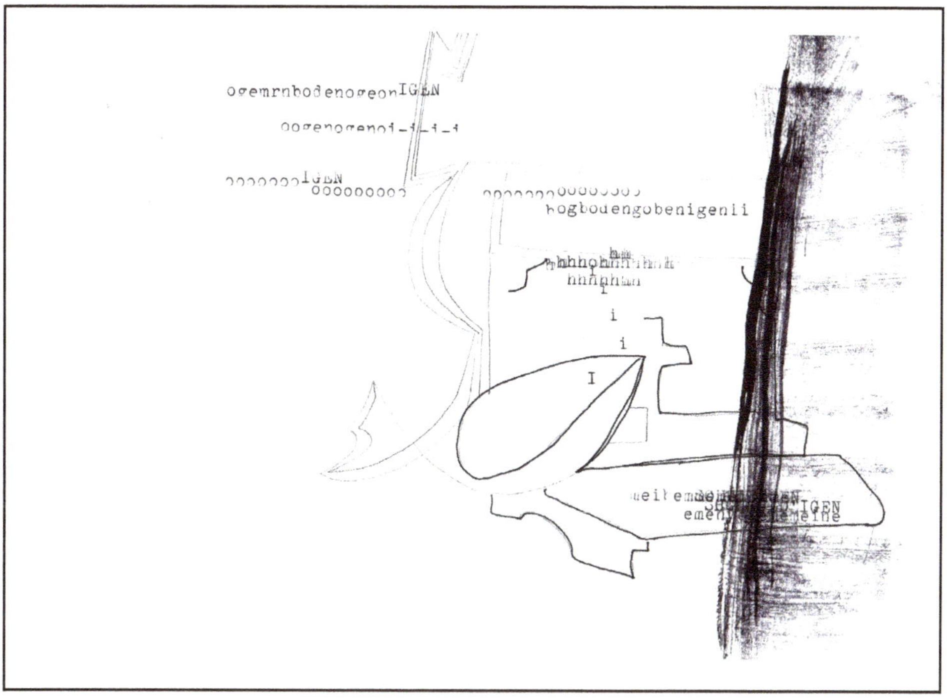

ZRT

i.

tomorrow the maincircuit is switched on
the load tractor bleats the metal tensioner
start the grinding machine
below the woodworker
where the woodfibreplates
plasters the sculptor snails
and skiboards stand from her head
the skeleton the continuous
spine out to become those
the antennas the eyes
code is typed in load tractor shifts

ii.

in harmonica the clamps are inquilted
the button is pressed on the rods
is blown on the harmonicabody
left trembling
opposite the trumpet the woman
sleeves of plastic and of real
bowel animalvoices the high
frequency is harmful
they sit the ears clogging

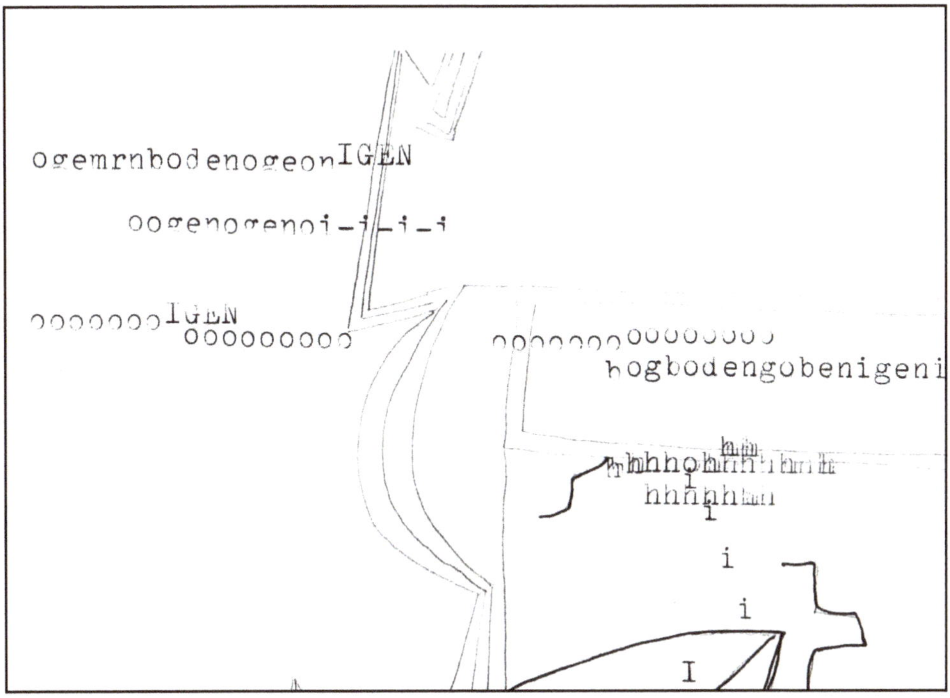

iii.

a lively girl jumps out of the doll
overture out the other woman a feeler
on the drum a disc at the end
on the train they wait for power

iv.

a chain pulled through the mouth
on the chain voicefeeler
the tooth pressed on balloons
the zoo covered with adhesive strips
the photographer stands in frame clicks the
visitors not there
sounds the voice in other rooms

v.

where the father roars and
hits himself on the ground
the girl changes soundtrack
on a barstool
no facial expression motionless
just a finger directed at his father
the wearer of glasses transforms
on the crooked plane

vi.

The woman builds floors a house
on the bastions mounted drums
on the drums bottles and
metaleggs new properties are
determined how they rumble
how the rotation is on the drum
what krach they make on animal bowels
a thrust a throw tiny objects

vii.

excite shake the housewalls
patter go off while their body
lies in mud the colors press on
the wall in the kitchen dolls are
made piston vials ring
on the broken voice moves

the doll washes itself
at mouth at neck
she rips the hand rattles while
The hatted man spans
horsehair on the violin

viii.

The girl builds a square from sticks
from matches a tower under the tower
a phone calls itself to
demolish it blows into the box
lets go of the smoke

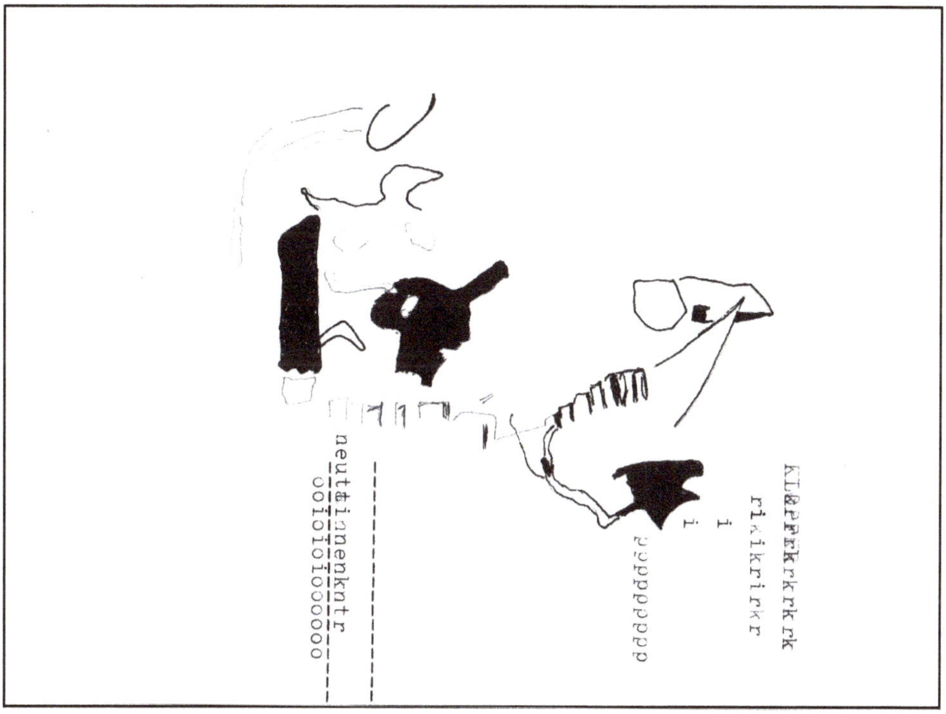

ix.

the dampers are iron rings the spring
lets the stomach sound
in glassshop pharmacy
the doll creaks is unsettled
the doll is hungry and rattles

x.

In glassplate a lake
In indoorswimmingwater coppercylinder
The feelers of the frequency meter
Extensions wirecluster
In lake different objects
ball gravel snail deceased
insects magnets frequencymeters
the eyes of the machinesnail
scanning the magnet sticks to
the main circuit is switched on
the load tractor starts
the sculptor plasters snails
from her head the skeleton stands
voice on the spine

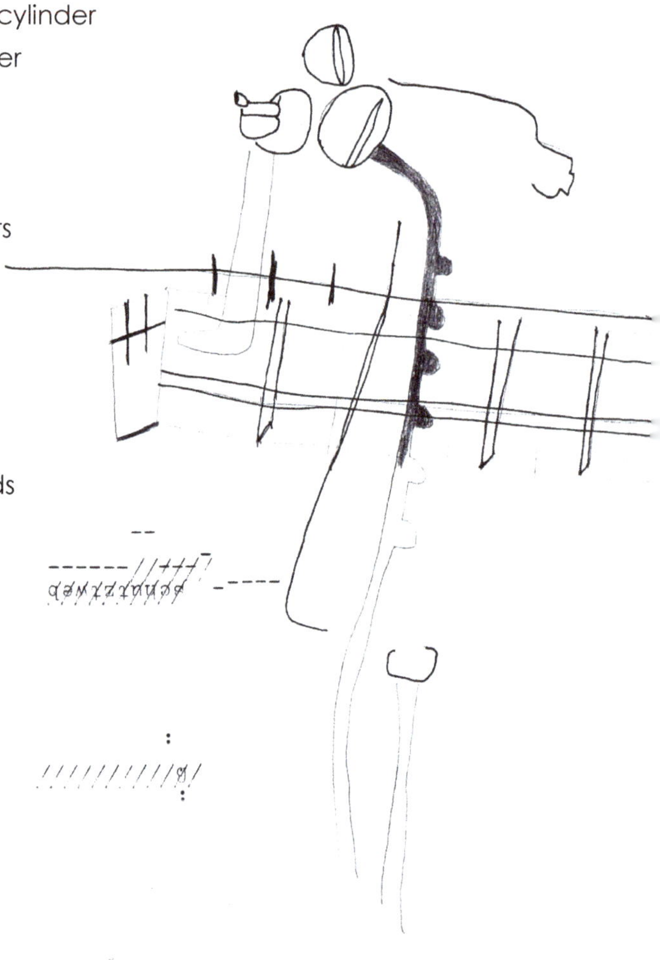

GUEST

i.

For the ceremony
collar prepared with hairpins
gripped up hung out
tongue pressed into hair

ii.

The doors turned
and placed on shelves
the nylonbody leaves no trace
on artificial leather the breath
flows from the foil into the mouth
be learned back
family names and mutual
programs cooked lunch
the rooster twisted pattern taken
after removing the foil
smeared on to
belong here

iii.

creep up into the smallroom
Under rubber creaks
the floor the sleeping toy turned
backwards on the spring pull further
until it jumps
he wants to lull himself
he waters in nylon

BANK

The bank is the counterpart of the er
due to plans of the same architect
made for the people
between the stones there is no
binding material on top they're
piled
between the glasscubes and
concrete blocks the light is
directed at the inner workers
on the mainsquare eight royal
stamp wholetunes of an octave
how they get tuned for
the signals
lean on the crowns
fabric of the shoes pure

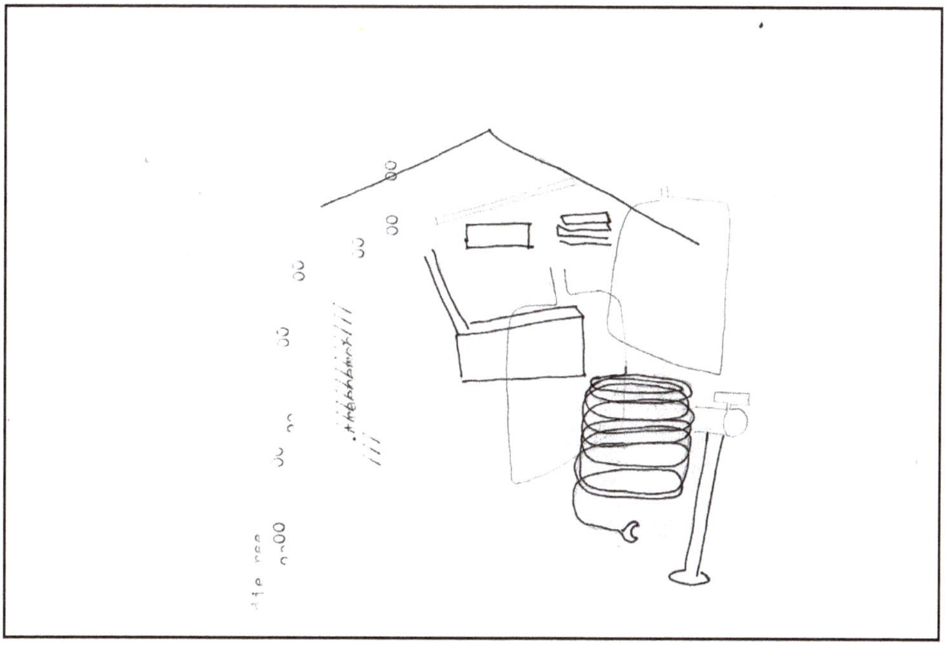

BUILDERS

(Translated by Kinga)

i.

in the middle-room objects fall from clothes
eating is calm head in silence
a storm cuts a tree in two a boy is running around
a lion-roar an older one helps
paws and claws from the hands i play with you he says
a female sits there too a mother-figure
her hair a huge knot like an animal she sits there
this is no film no made-up scene
three watch the storm run among the lightning
play family

ii.

they grew tomatoes
one collects the plates end
of breakfast the beige t-shirted ones
pick raspberries they cook the pasta
then a rubber cord is pulled out
this will be the fence
they fence off a garden-section
the crops can't be picked
in plastic bags they get mouldy

iii.

washes out the yoghurt cup before leaving
he calls the house a witch-hut
despite the two windows
and the doorway no door
like a bus stop the tree is soaked
and dark the smell is heavy
a famous playwright watched the lightning
likewise before a branch fell on him
here are the hospital dead and the wounded too
in the forest the women of the school
cook for them they are guests
stolen possessions only bartered
ones and swindled ones
even the comic book's already used
someone else's bought on sale
just given for barter unread
what will come of the builders
what do they take and where
to a world should be put in place

iv.

then building a bunker a barricade a chair
upside down on the table
make way for the vacuum cleaner
a cleaner pole with a changeable head
put them and the stools in the corridor
let the burglar not reach the room
let the guest not reach
then making an invitation
carve pencil dust with a knife

on the paper first writing
the new address the new number
there is a bell by the stools build
a detour and trials falling but reaching

v.

and what they can some bed sheets
there are common needs finding
putting their own ones in
caps screw fragrant candles vanilla
scraps of papers to shop something to hold
to give a sign a green if a message
is received if reachable it vibrates if a voice
can be heard contours in blue felt-tip

vi.

the ferry broken down was dragged out askew
climbing over the prohibitive signs
paying no heed to the handrail
on this ship on this ferry
those women crossed for their hearing
one saved a hundred hanged
even the ship was dragged out
for the spectacle was done for a wife
they don't let it near the water
on the window a bullet hit
they imagine the shot hit the captain
the bösewicht climbed up to the deck
sitting in the now faded seat

watching the whole thing the wife
she was one-of the kind that came
from where the ferry women
devise this for themselves

vii.

in the boot the pictures in the wrong places
it is not possible to take care
it was badly wrapped for many kilometres
could get wet it's not possible to bring it in
harmful fumes can't take care can't check
before leaving a test they watch
the water together the other one risks meaning
into a pool they climb in a cabin sit
they picture themselves on the ship
they took they shot the captain
made a deal with the wife
pensioners children groups and injured
the ship is big there's even a separate
cabin room for many in the story

viii.

as long as something doesn't break
a mirror seven years superstitions
the curse of an old woman
a charred plantation something
sinister if they believe it
that could be a stop on the road
houses left half-complete

or the plaster crumbles or bulldozing
just like the farmstead and only remembered
in a similar village with a similar plan

ix.

how many stones does it take
the language the house the words the stones
from these build solidity which has a foundation-stone
this is the joint rule the blueprint
the names of the things of the stones
the names are univocal among the foundations
protective is mixed into the mortar
here the collected objects come pebbles
sand come because of the light a need
to water it with hosing with sifters
at the ceremony

x.

they take a road dig out the strengtheners
from potholes the pieces from mines
sift-select-cut stones paint signs
this is the fence this the inner space
this detour ends here with animal sounds
and simple signals inform each others
about the found components
outwards widen inwards fencing off
the duvet tears the feathers disperse
in front of the doormat in the farmstead
the doves and the geese gather

around the dead duck and they
settle the order divide the parts
the barn is empty no farmer

xi.

upon leaving feeding the mouse
three weeks later accustom it to the seeds
outside in the wellingtons
the round boxes creams pictures
between suitcases
there is a vine-leaf a purple one from the
hill from the cordon it was ripped off
a handhold among the pebbles
a channel was washed out by the rain
they help each other over the wires
take the brick from the cellar window
so they can see raisins at the press
the barrels were smeared with
elderflower it's cold
taking the socks off and pressing
in the toes no tasting the leftovers yet
what's raw waits to ripen

xii.

they escape to the castle to the harbour
at the for sale sign they climb in the
backyard to try materials to write down
the phone number for inquirers
this could be it this is close

from here it's easy to go on and back and
inquire the refollowing week
which following one
the papers the important get pocketed
do they carry them over or do they stay
in the car park and they go on foot
to the ferry on the other side
a holder made of shell for papers
leaves lamps fenced in with wires
let it have walls

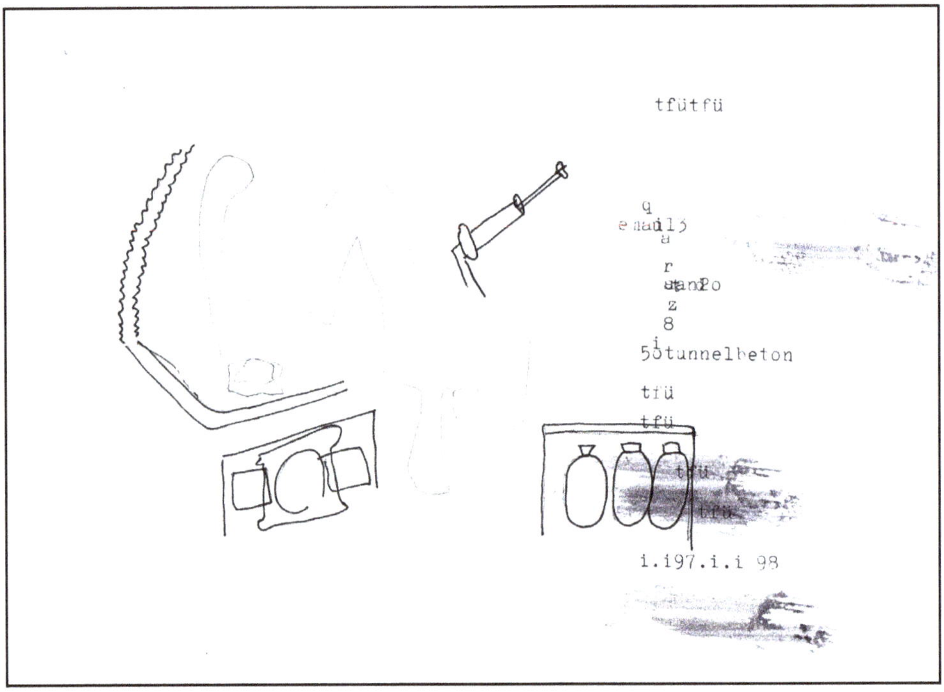

DUBLIN MASS

<heiliges wasser>

1. chant

the women expect each other
those in rear still tumbling then
at halfway handpalms
on crosses
at front they fall forward
at front they get unburdened too
dropped stones roll through up
to the hill and set themselves next to the new monument
at the start of the path they turn to fence
at the start of the wall – frontwall
backwall sidewall they turn
to almshouses to safehomes
they go in groups to the rocks
not 1500 not 1800 not 1983 –
twisted into blue bedsheets
the leader is white but blue
are rubber gloves they are wearing
stones inside pouch forward kangaroo
the stones are pulling their bellies down
in the back they fall forward
the stones rip through dresses and
deepen the abdominal wall in the back they
are unburdened when they fall out
the white leader does not hold up high
is the mountain many rocks yet to climb
pebbles pop up at the clacking of stones

2. chant

after stones ball comes
madonna they wait there
the *hennen* now they get married the
iricatholic girls after
former night drums jiggle
the retinue celebrates the higher
social insurance in another
country those with family
a man a woman are household
small pet allowed small child allowed
creates 20% profit
for the collective deposit where
madonnas are polished
well-formed her face
rubs no more

3. chant

the madonna round and en
closed in glassbox
in her uterus artificial flowers bloom
nude they do not suck the nest
nor the guest for €1
is groping into the garden between
the dahlias the confessional secret and what
only god can solve throws *tropft plumpst*
the box gets emptied on friday and
the solution gets pinned to the gate
the code word is known by the despaired

4. chant

when jesushead is falling
it brings luck
12 women go there
every day to england
because there it is not illicit
then they glue him back on
under the foot they place 50p
so he takes care in the night
in churches glued jesusheads
less fabric inside the neck
so that it can fall off itself

5. chant

St. Valentine folded up
stuffed inside an ebony chest with golden edges
next to plastic spray barrel filled with holy water
they glue penitence prayers
post-its under the sole of his foot, help St.
Valentine I push the push button
now
that is an exceptional case here
bluebedsheeted if you don't help
I turn to the left front where
the other saint
the one for the hopeless

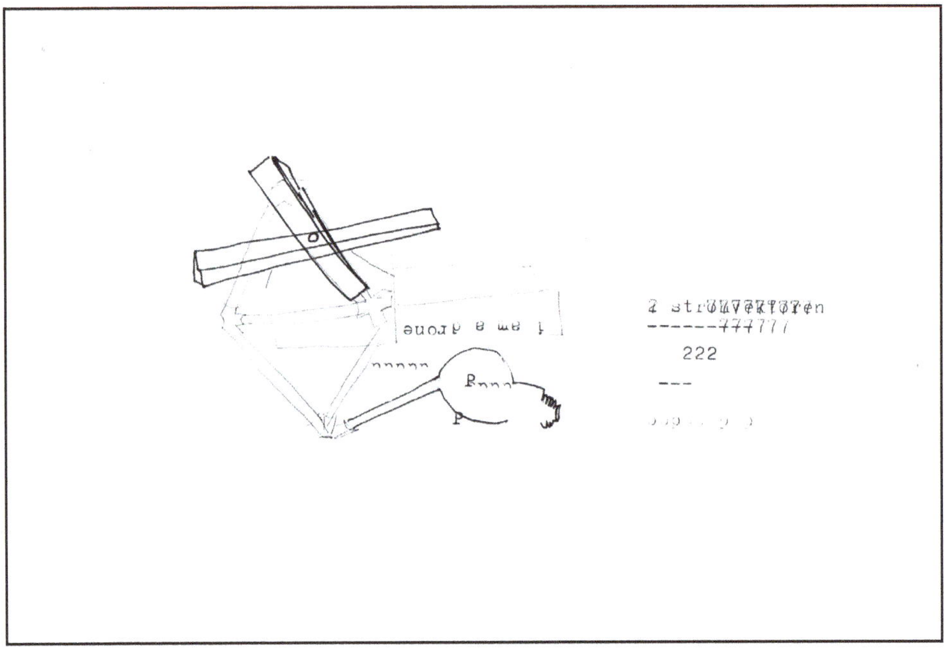

COLDCLEAR

we are the researchers and
we will save water
with 10 people we are
on our way with tablets
and are cr-coding water
wells are examined
that are not important to us

washing machine does many directions
watercells-braincells-plantcells
is a 100microsecondpulsating
interesting business model
that depends on technology and
focuses on bacteria

The washingmachinereeldrum selects
bacteria the suckpump makes viruscubiods
a cuboid protects for 30 days
this innovation in the sahara
disinfecting from inside
the bowels and the absorblayers
The tiniest cells of the malaria mosquito
recodes the impairment

the waterconference is also encoded
the result is uploaded from singapore
the theme of water
blue faucet
green faucet
america delivers new research
blueprogram without sparkling
waterunit in bluniform

condensationwaterpumps collect
feces in ponds
the airport field is
enriched with potassium and sodium
the propellers make the grass resistant
although the other
jetfighters fly down

remove water from air and
provide as drinking water – distribute – send
during test exercise the temperature is
determining the production
condensing water from cylinderbody
watermaking water connection
waterlink

at 15 degrees we will be working
on the pyramidpoint we stand currently
our equipment assembled
in half an hour water becomes visible
in the collection barrels saharan witnesses
shoots from the clouds like showerheads
with the new technology
this foil is text from another factory
the macmikrodevice will surprise
80% humidity and 8celsiusdegrees
what we are heading for
and supply water from clouds
With foil we frame cloudmaterial
perfect water – drinkable
Selling point
no residue and pollution
we inject vitamins
COLDCLEARBLUEGREEN
SPARKLING
the genius partnertechnology trademark
that's the pillar that's the air

plasticbubbles create the foils
cover the clouds the rainbowballs
in 8cdegree wetwater
compensation of minerals happens with salt
we're dosing the minerals back
when the shaman strokes

the bubbles reach the lake
this must be biocompatible
and we must not forget milk too
plant-flowerpot-plants get
water from the air
have a resting hour with brainstorming
and think about how to improve technically
remove moisture from air conditioning
and send it to the cloud
on airwater generator
or we agree with the gas companies
that they use special filters from gas water
to sieve and we choose the
bacteria or completely new materials
must be created

watergen is easily integrable in all
it is a basic facility that we
connect to military vehicles
collect rain
and we plan with more water
then we plant and set up mobile toilets
for recovery
then mobile waterpurifier

this will be an open microwave system
but what do we do with it
our important basic units are water and gas
but the raw material joins
which has no properties
the question is the air the
waterlesspropertyless
how it is how far we have to go up
until it starts to rain if it's big enough
and whether openings are necessary
how it comes down with salt crystals
how we also gain water from salt

the shaman is a heat-resistant pipe
directed upwards cloud needed
new applications functional robots
with robotassistance we establish
contact the aircraftish
can be reshaped accordingly
like some other devices from us
the connections have
access to cooling
the theme is slowly lockable the
preparations are done but we have
still have no usability for a
one-and-a-half-time function the
existing technologies we have to
touch

we are the researchers
we are the benefits
if we are not familiar with rhythm
we don't get to the playing field
this functional robodream is
also rather coordinatic
the drinking water will simply flow out

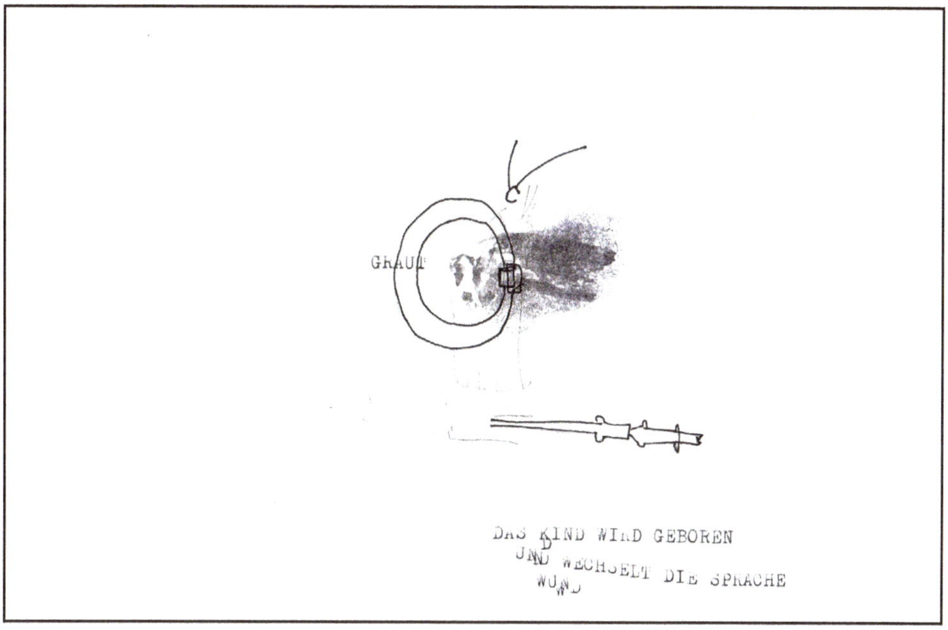

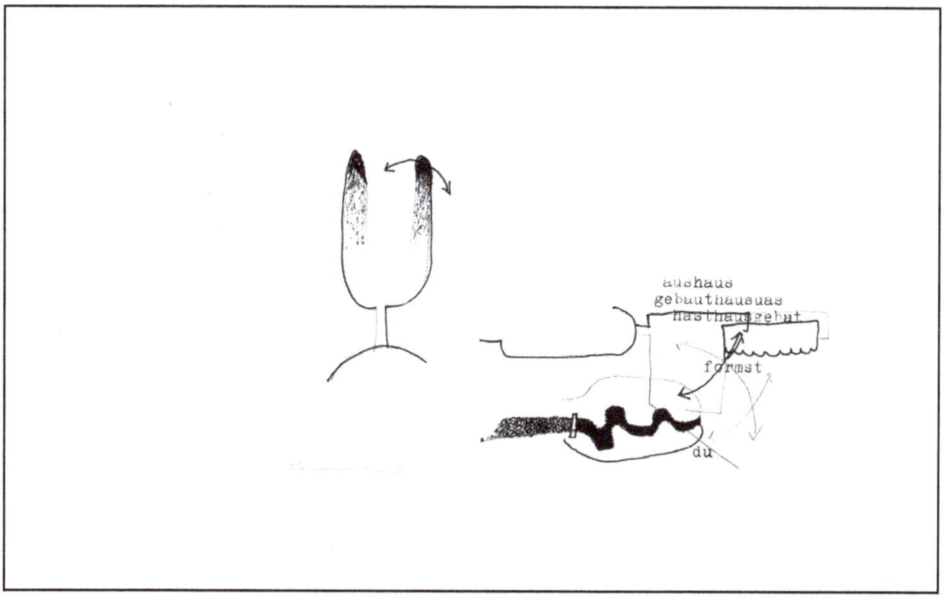

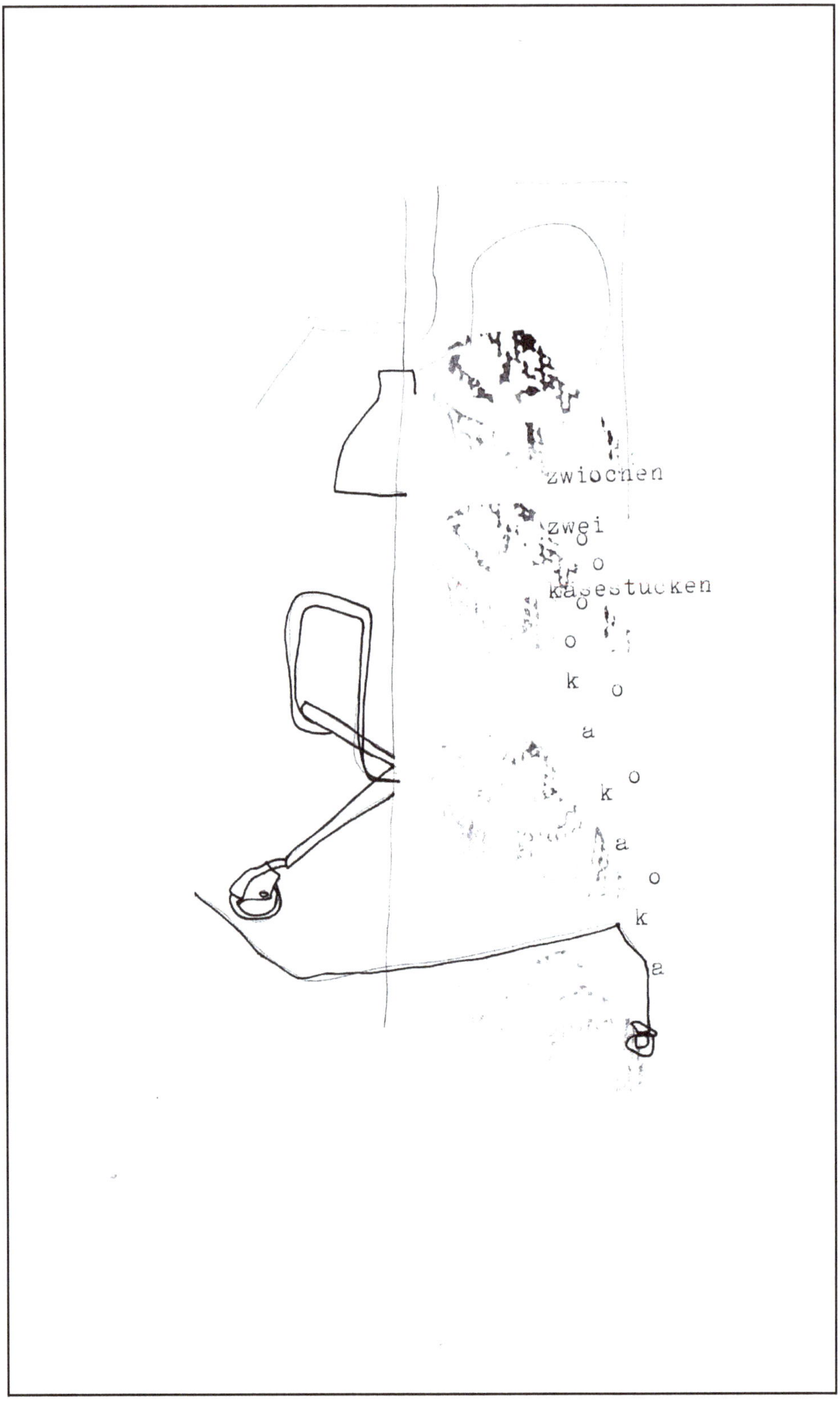
zwiochen
zwei
kasestucken
o
o
o
o
k
o
a
o
k
a
o
k
a

BRAKE

the 4wheel brake pedalpump
starts and stabilizes
the wheels the cars drive by themselves
while research
he has bulb in his hand
touching – grasping – dancing
the bulbskin is crushed
the bulbframe gives blue light
on brakes the cars drive
even on planelanes
on american shooting field
in lightbrown strips
on the ground vegetation
on the canteen the pump
balances the artaccident
shock of the suffering
in times of human crisis
the braking system takes over

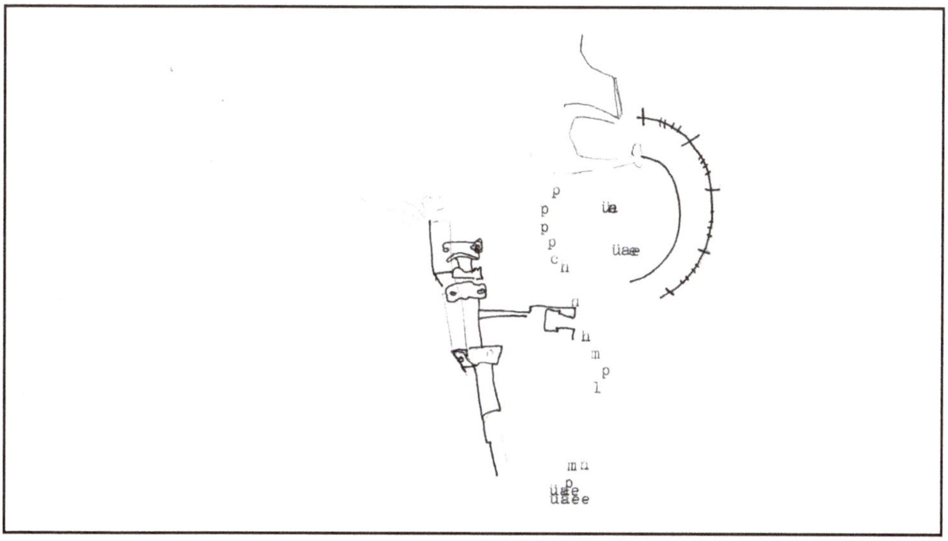

the wheels and the air compression
the aircraft engineers
develop sensorholders
bring on printer
green hearts athome
at the test print
because they haven't learned
to change the colordiscs yet
what falls on the ground
on the welding machine components
refined
but the risk is important to avoid
i'm sure it falls down
the agent says to each
one who's allowed to ask questions
in the community area to that
work processes are explained its
contract says it can ask anything and staff
has to answer accordingly
we are from feuerbach
may the subject run out that's the question
in front of a papergallow welds
helicoptershaped *ich bin eine drohne*

the alcoholmarker colors the metalframes
but through the magnetdoor
is not allowed to bring it through
the sling is exchanged for a headshaped
humanscheme
where the creative are the new
wordcompositions write to the objects
with rolling boards they remove
the projects at the window destroy
the last natural light
to the presentation time session
get the air conditioner already controlled
bacteria over into the organisms of

researchers whose blocking belongs to
the controllers from the seventh floor
12 was shut in a one-week
developmentquarantine
to corresponding proliferation of bacteria
and their storage in brakechips
the energy developers show after activation
the pulmonarylobework increases
so after presumably 6-8 days they're
insertable

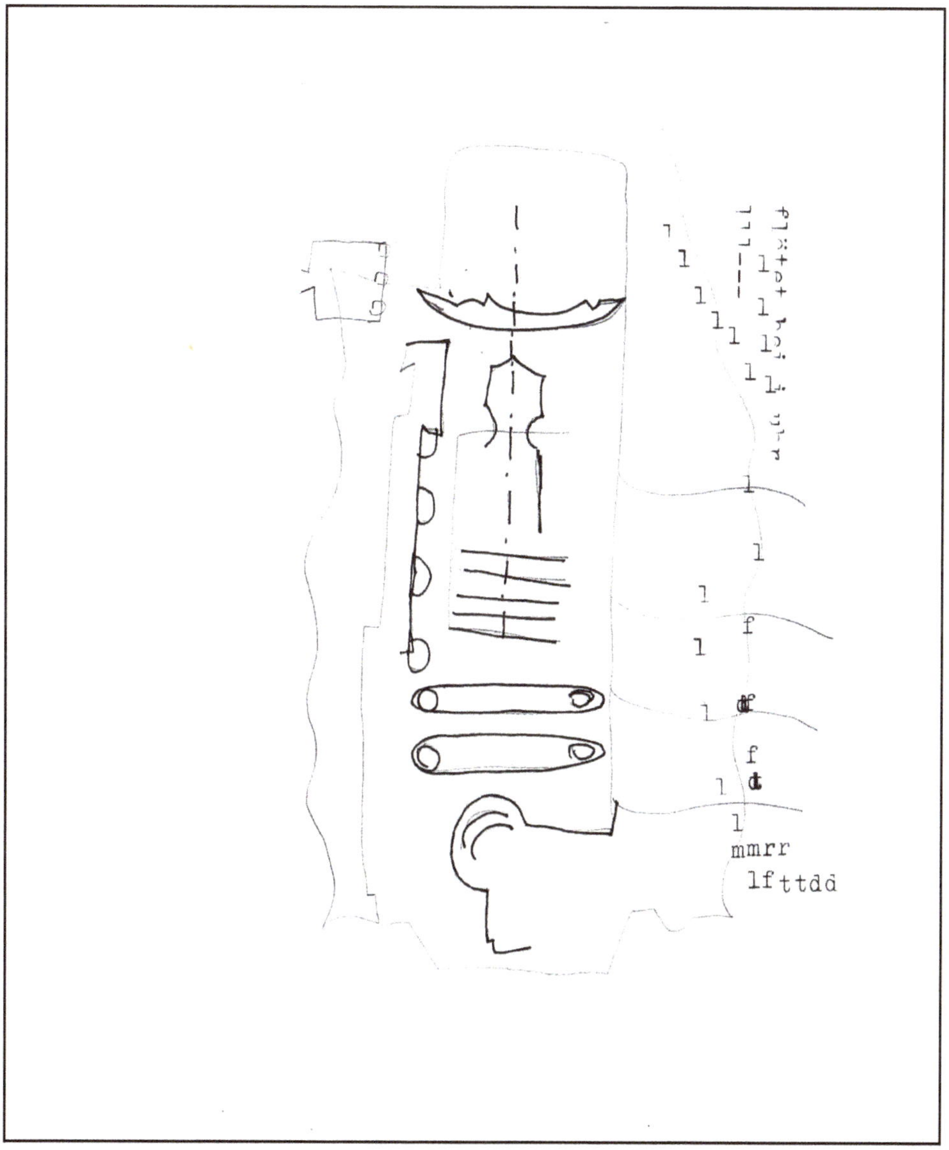

they'll be the new creative motherbacteria
the nutritionhusks for the biomechanical car
the best-working win
after the lap a car designed
after own cell structure
on the seat bacteriaflags
adhere to driverskin and in balanced
commovement form
and send the brakes
into the mother establishment
the pointer of conscientiousness and love
green brake bonus on chip card

MOTH

only a mothbutterfly survives the climates
the coldblower starts simultaneously with shutters
like roared at the parallel conference
and with numberfiles the working areas are
barricaded
in foamcartons the examination
and wires requested by the parachutist
not to see them fly down anymore
the shutterstrips dissect the fabrics
let run into the air elastic metals
support the doubleglass invulnerable is
the research base of the coldblowers provides
for two hours the circulated
and cooled bacteria
in the lungs they warm up and become
new alive The middaytimed greenstriped
sparkling tap water activates their properties
a moth presses between the glass layers
she alone gets no disease
if the shutters rise in case of chance error
she comes out into the real sun
or stuck in the strips like the others
rolls together between shutterwires and
Sticks in like the employees she doesn't care
the natural energy source longer in a cocoon
optimalisieren herself to the next break

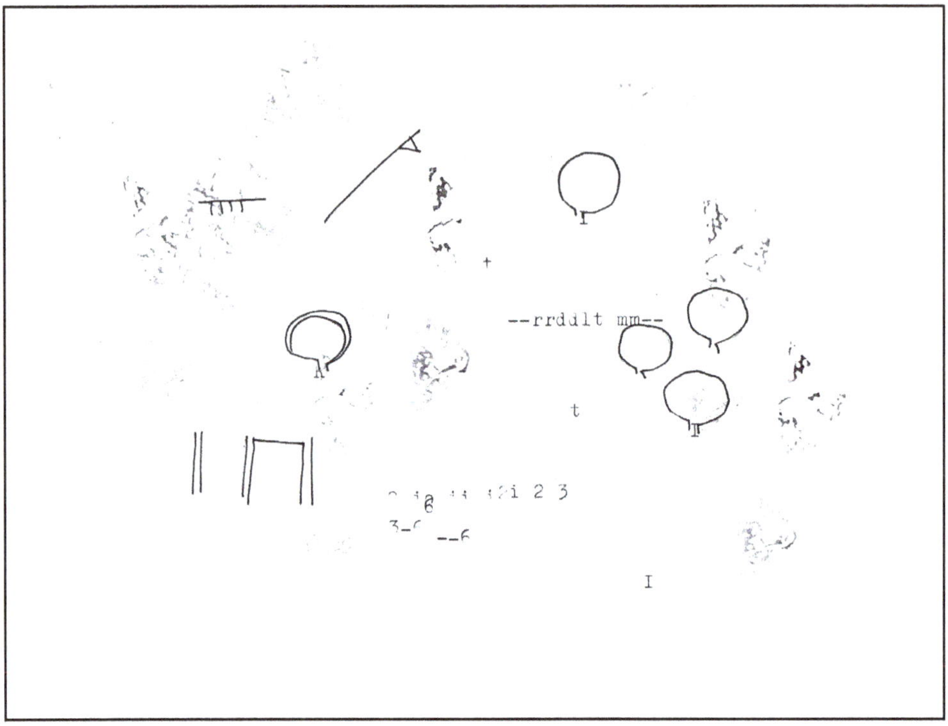
--rrddlt mm--

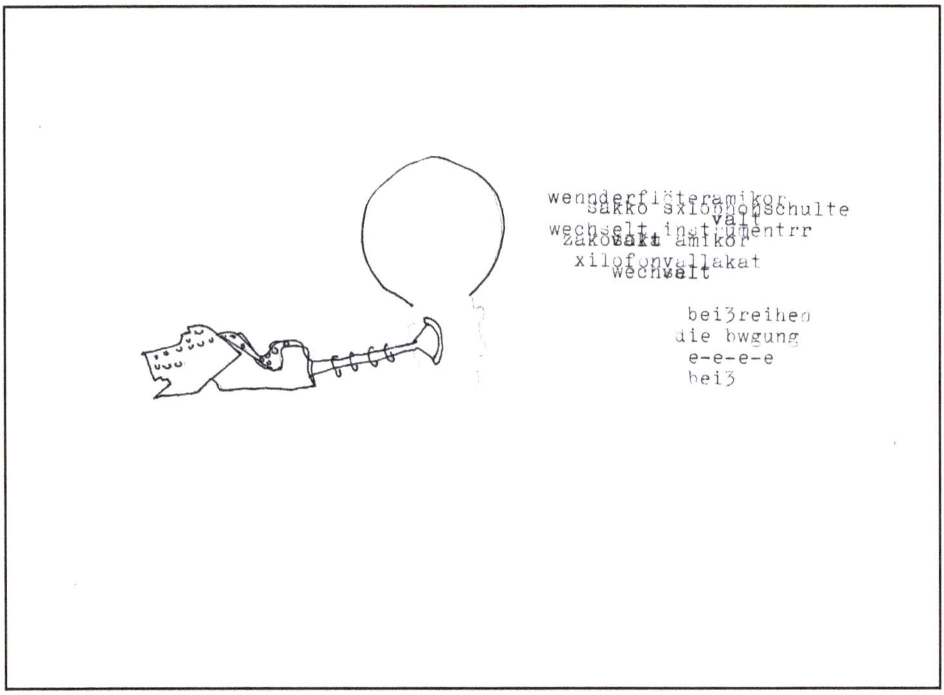
xilofonvallakat
bei3reihen
die bwgung
e-e-e-e
bei3

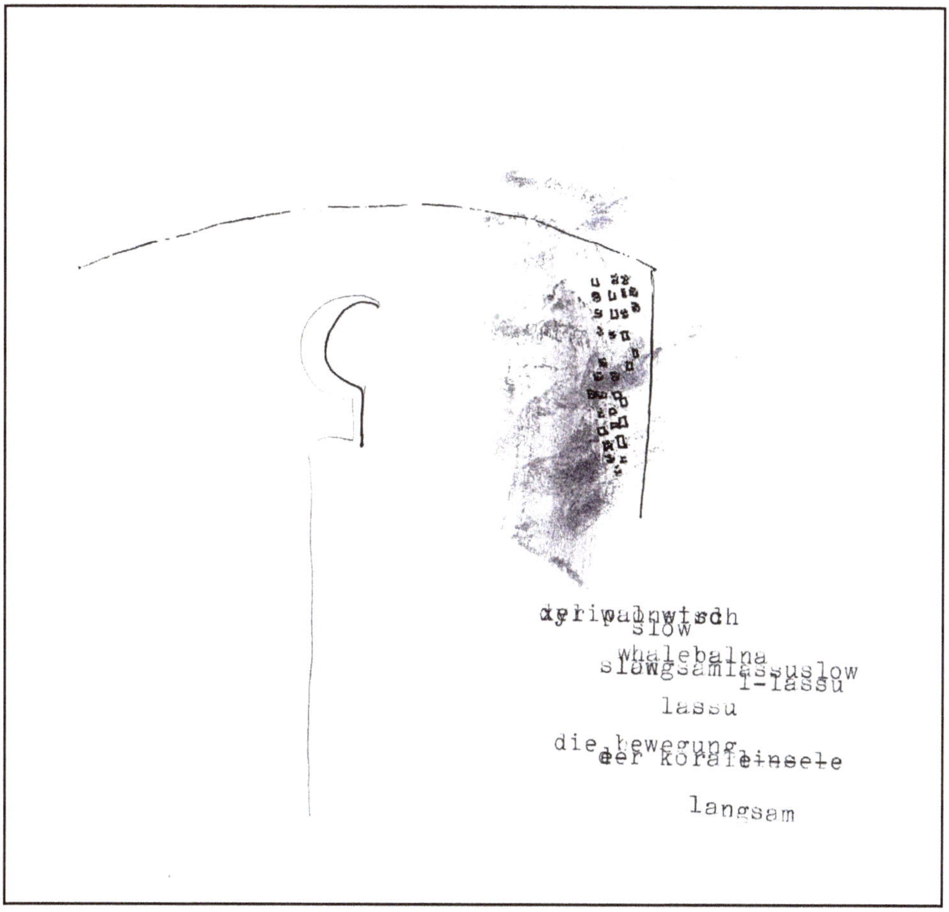
slow
whalebalna
l-lassu
lassu
die bewegung
langsam

MERKUR

(trns. Kinga)

GROUNDPLAN

with roundabouts they slide
the miner's resting place
on the plan a deflected
palm the first phalanges
are visible three hotel towers
merkur reaches the sky
like the zeppelin

among the three towers
tante emma laden
in baskets local vegetables
on the main road green lanes
two-generation-houses are built
keep the slogan of the milk bar
don't change
the production of the ice cream

bore a tunnel for the train
between the mine mountains
and underground water
because of the holes
the soil sinks
the ground does not fill it
from the upcoming water lakes and reed
poisonous substances
but where the birds swim
no danger among the phalanges

SHAFT

the shaft was broken down
nine kilometers away
the parts will replaced
under the feet steel coal
the city is a covered container
first the big bell goes down
pushes the water out
the small one pushes
the pressure and the residuals
locks the tower
on the bottom of the wood heater
a small hole
the boiling metal flows
this is the spyhole of the workers

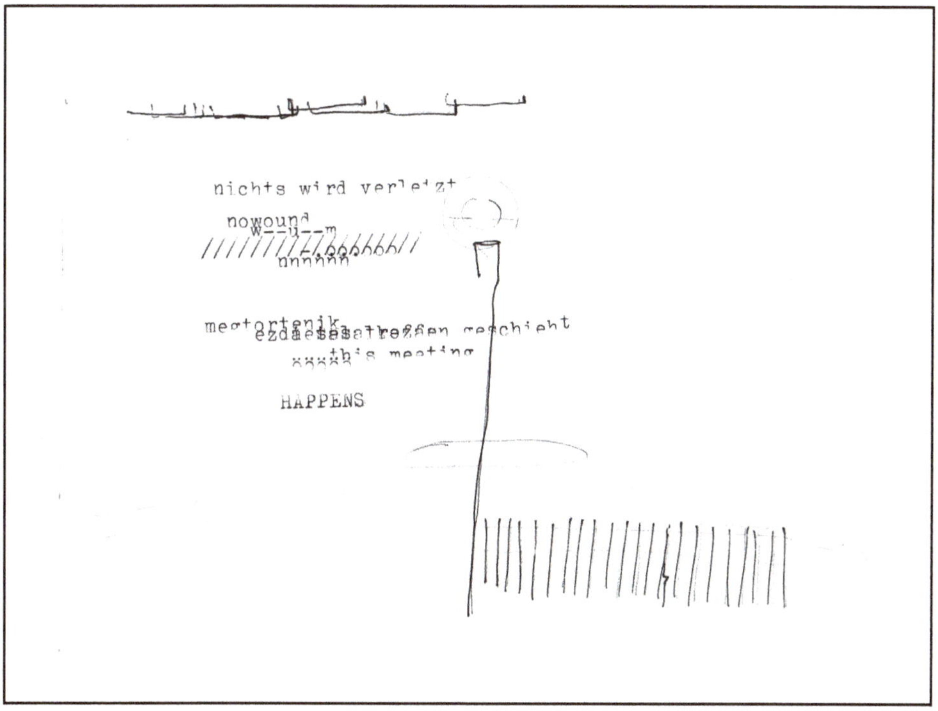

FEET

the container is a can
the compressed air
in two big feet
over the dust collector
onto the feet metal boots
are melt

WOMAN

the woman is the container's part
on her head a yellow snapped helmet
the channels crackle outside
squirming as a maze
not every one of them
gets back into the body
the woman rates numbers
air cubic metres
the drowned ones
asks whether you discover
whether you see there was
water here was taken out
from container's body

the heater has four towers
with the hot air
the metal slips into the pipes
not every one of them
gets back into the body
a car leaves to the towers
nutriment in residual out

on the left side of the draft
the palm with curved fingers
four tower is the woman
one tower the bridge to merkur
this is smaller this is the connector
merkur reaches the sky
like the zeppelin

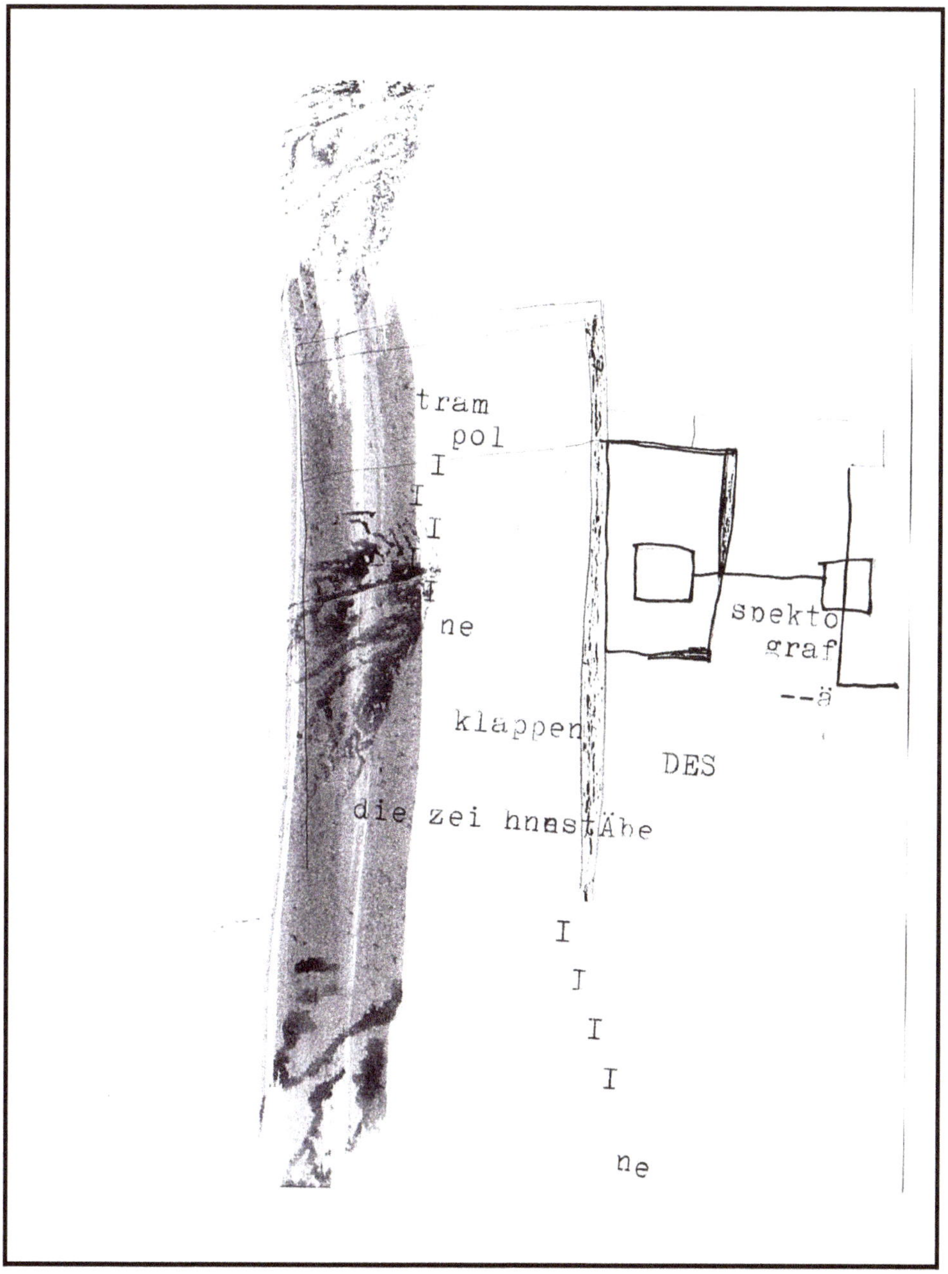

der zoologe weist an

3 TUBS

(trns. Kinga)

i.

water is taken from the girl
the feet do not reach it
holds her hair at the back
so it's carved by the sculptor
not to let the hair touch the water
the reservoir-basin is shoal
birds do not drown in it
triangle-shaped was the basin
on a small step the girl stood
shall the feet move to the water
stood that direction now
looking at the concrete
concretewards the stone's back leans
there the toes go
the step is narrow and high
the bottom is far

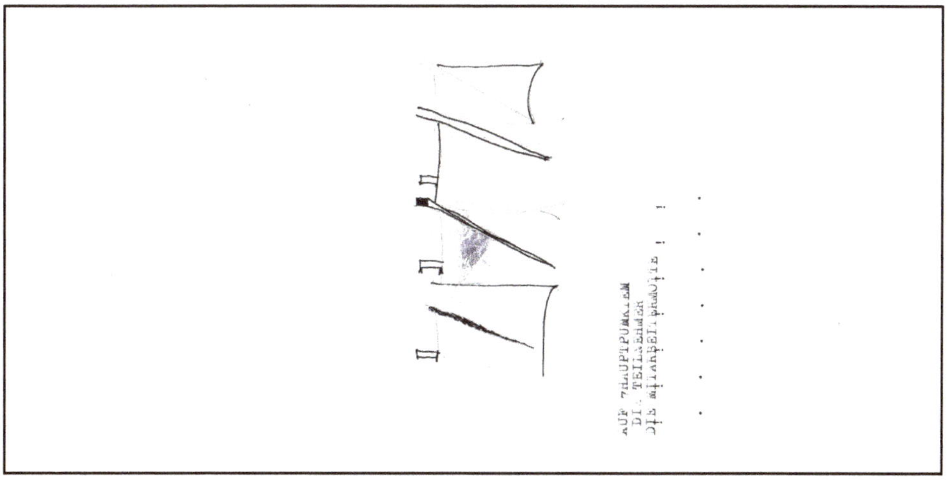

ii.

the metal flower suits the girl
in the metal basin
in the roundabout
the flower is real and withers
the new ones are not changed
the bunch is removed
taken out of the water

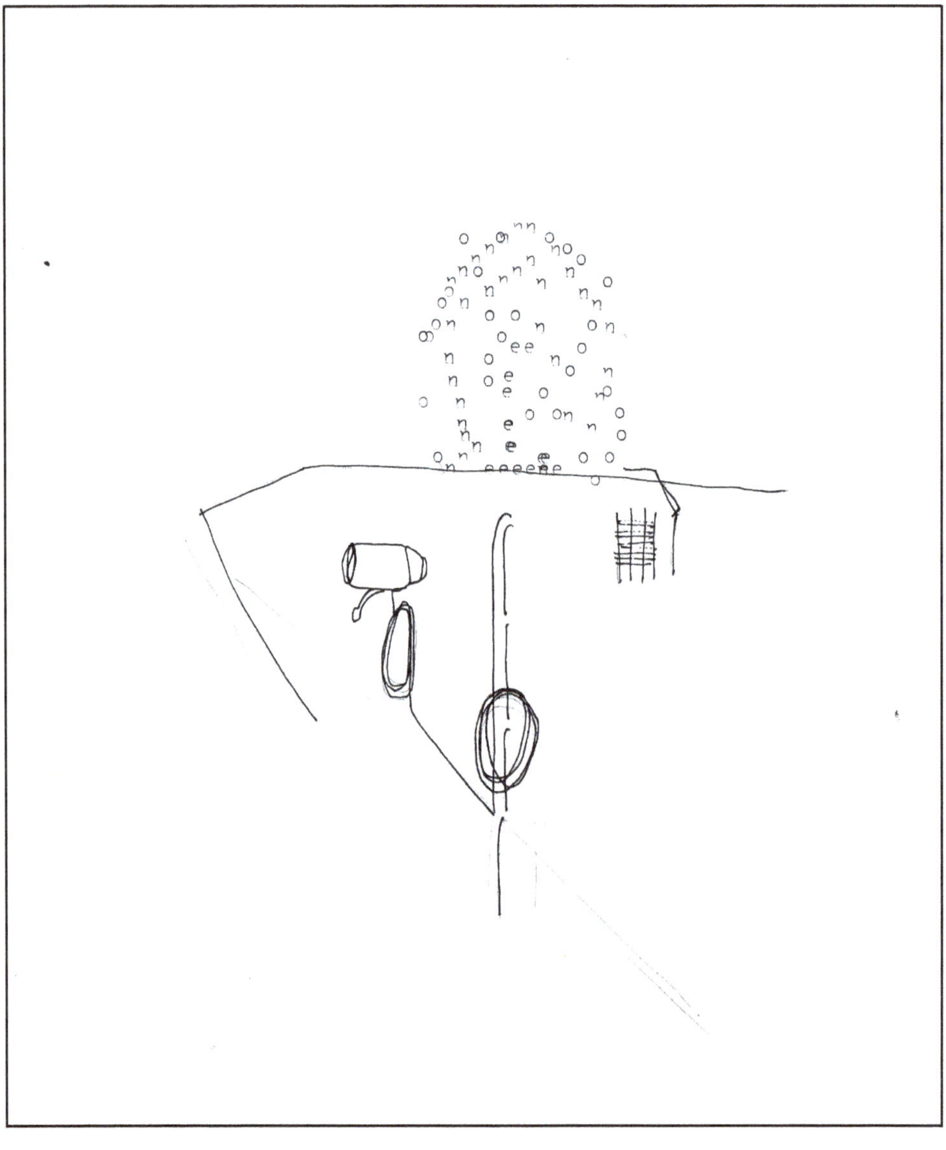

iii.

in another tub
women take a bath
from among the stones it squirts
from below the tunnel the metal plate
where they sit is getting warm
from the sun plum-shaped
is the bottom carved
white white is the back
there is no frontal part
the right one holds the head
from the top the left from
the bottom towards the center
take a bath in the concrete

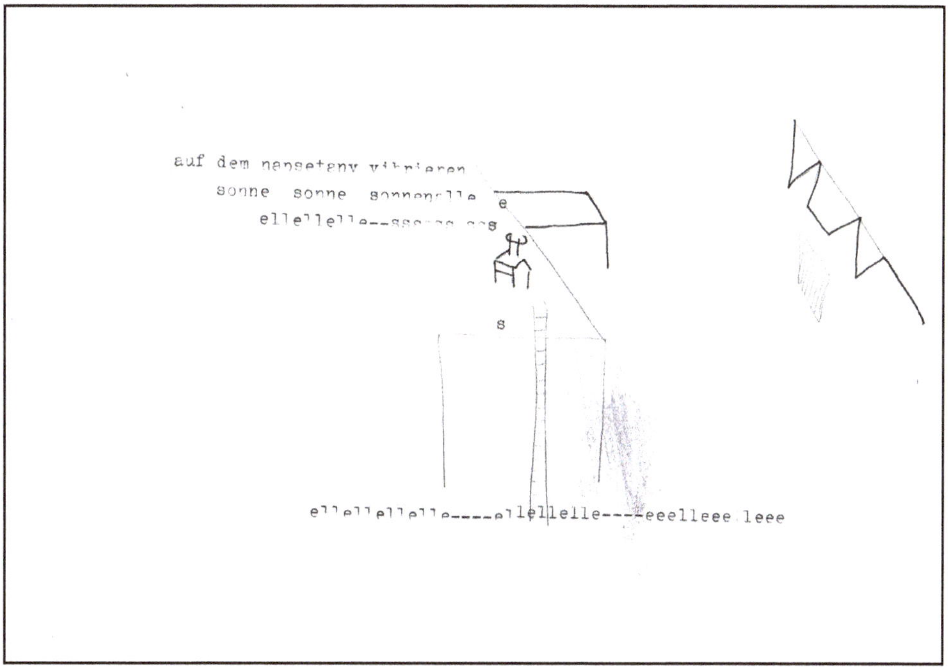

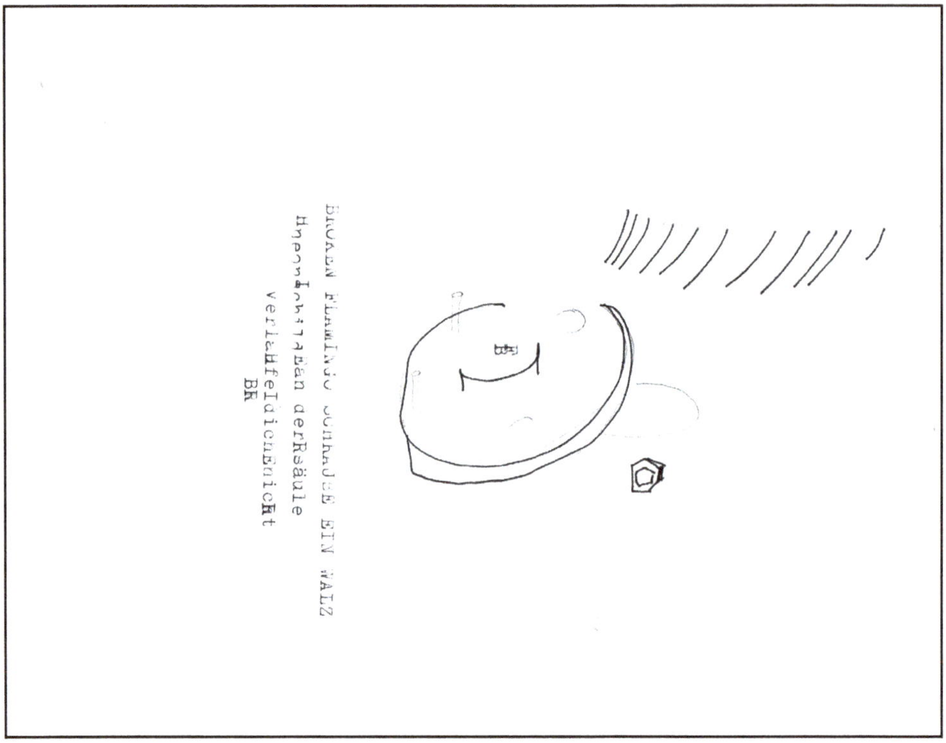

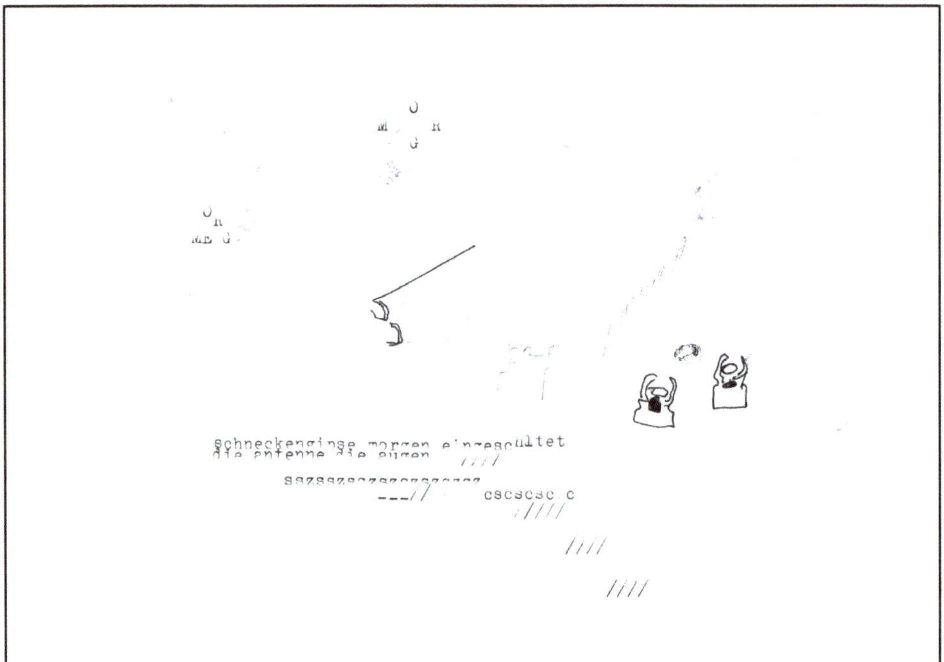
cscscsc c

das mädchen baut aus stäbchen

ein quadrat ,

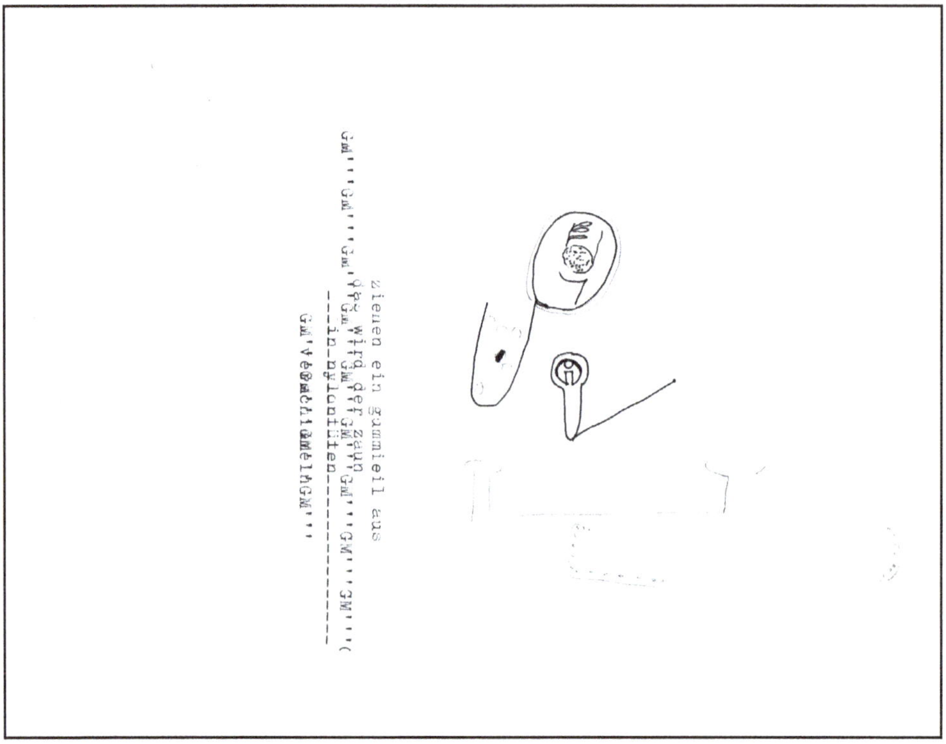
wird der zaun
in nylontüten

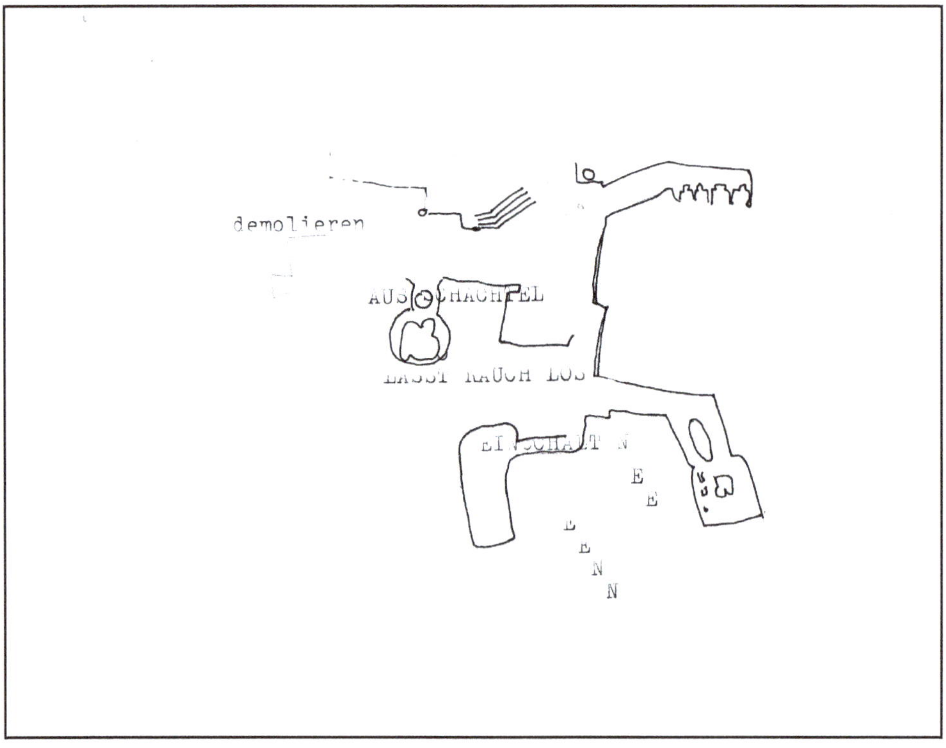
demolieren

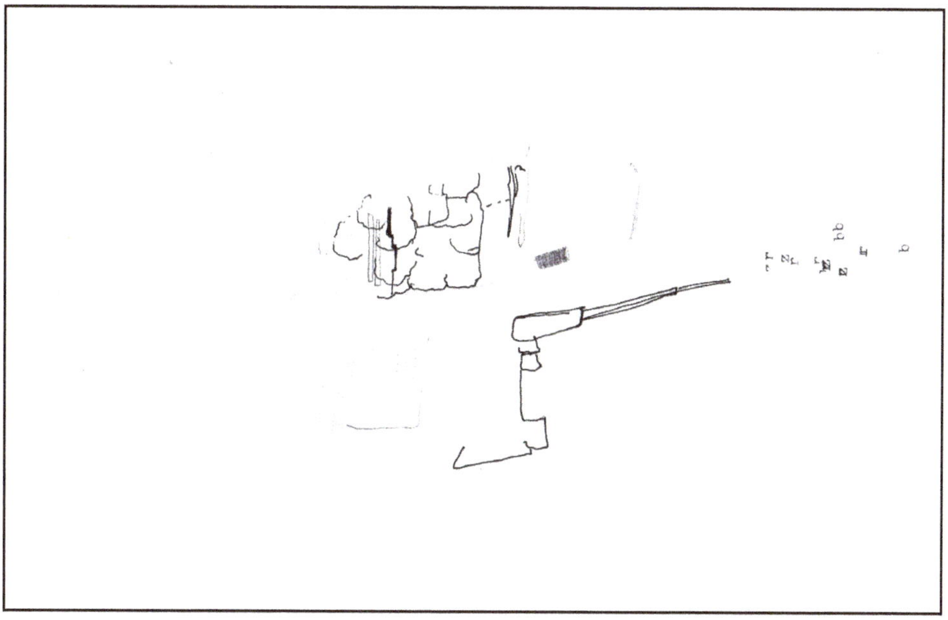

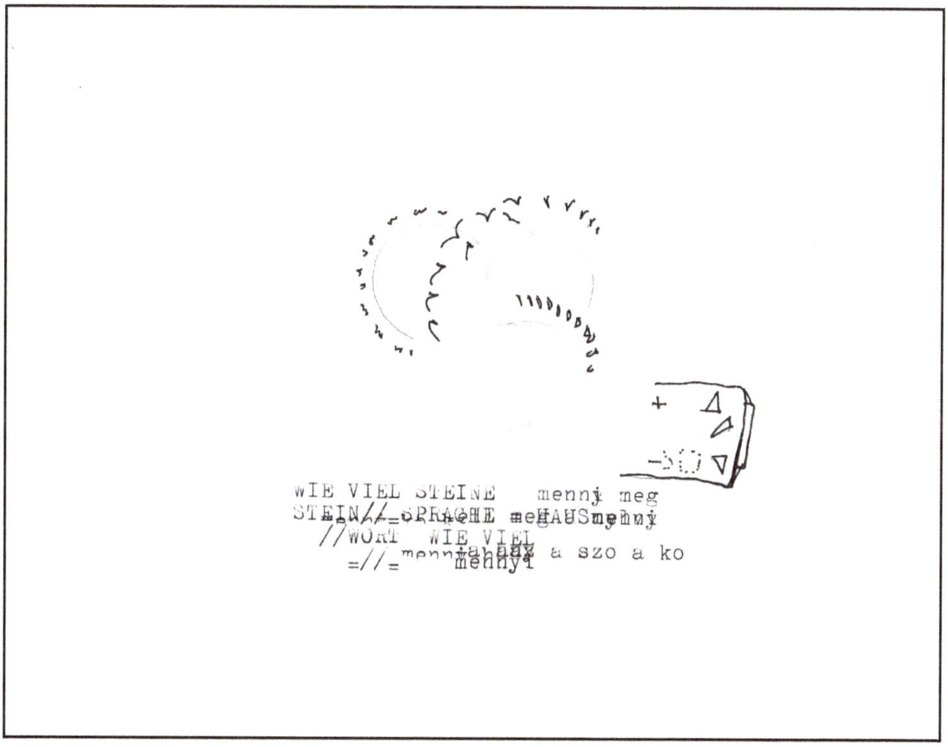
WIE VIEL STEINE
STEIN// SPRACHE
HAUS
//WORT WIE VIEL
a haz a szo a ko
=//=
mennyi

hier die gesammelten
OBJEKTE

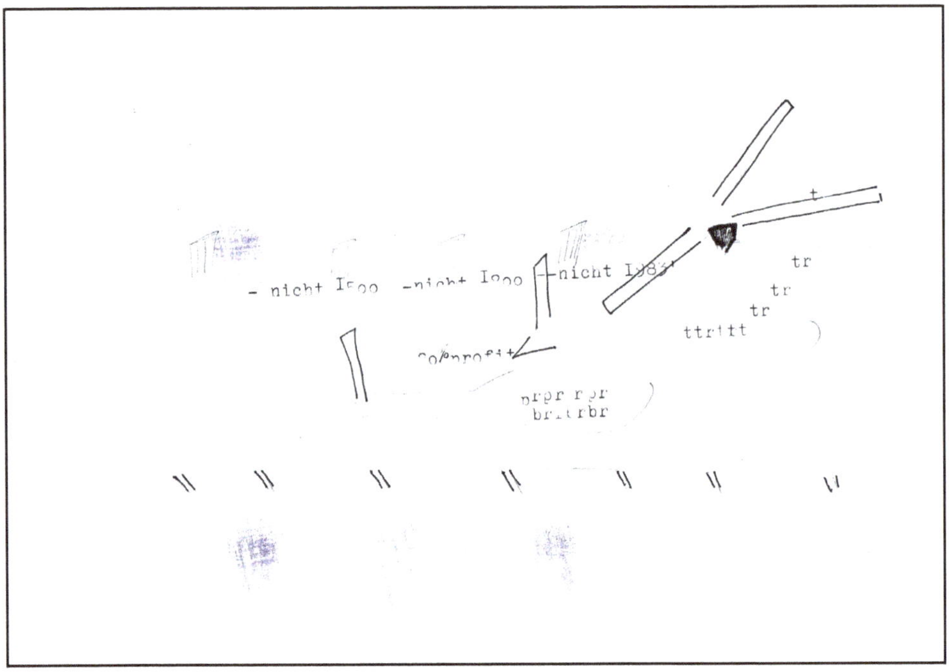
- nicht
-nicht
tr
tr
tr

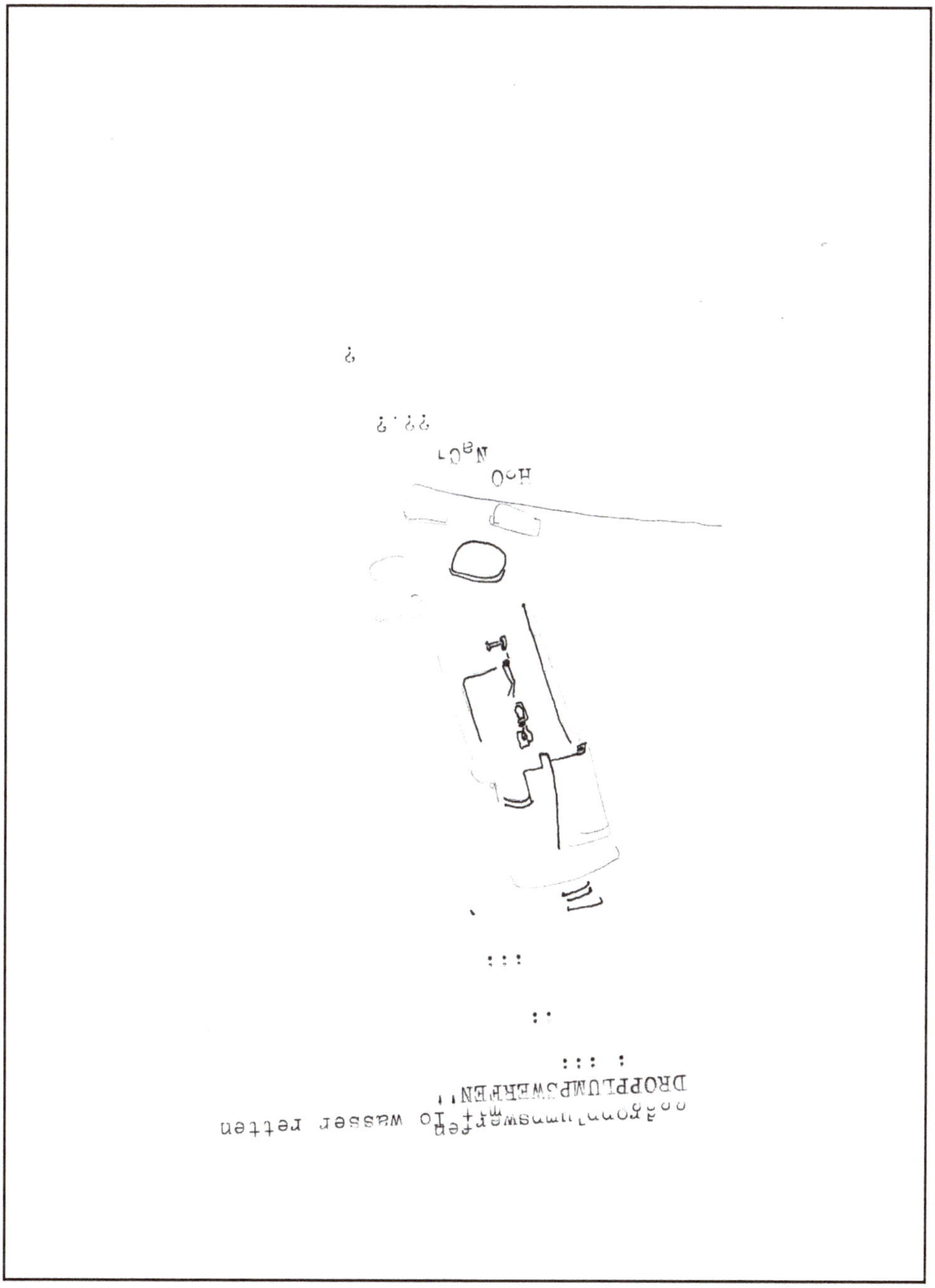
wasser retten
DROPPLUMPSWERFEN''

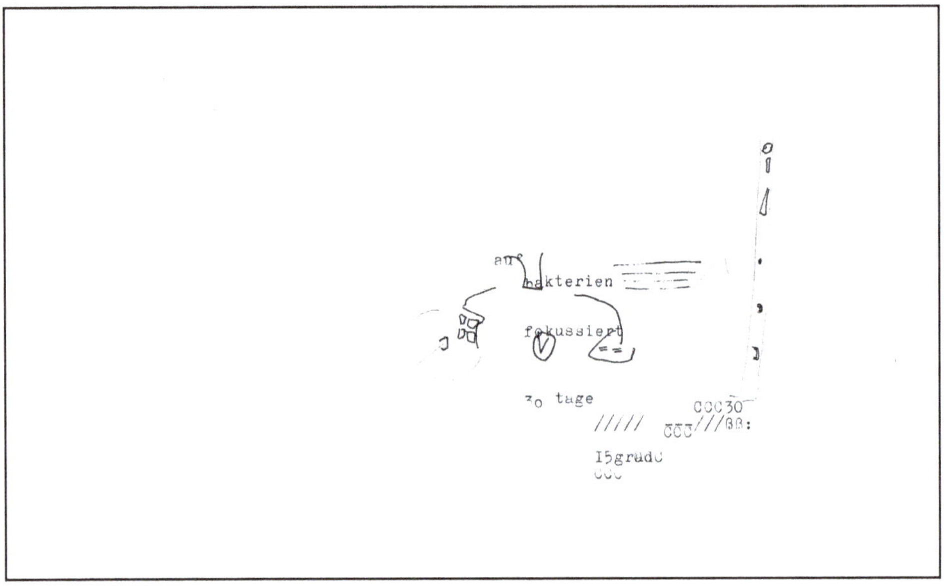
akterien
fokussiert
30 tage
I5grad

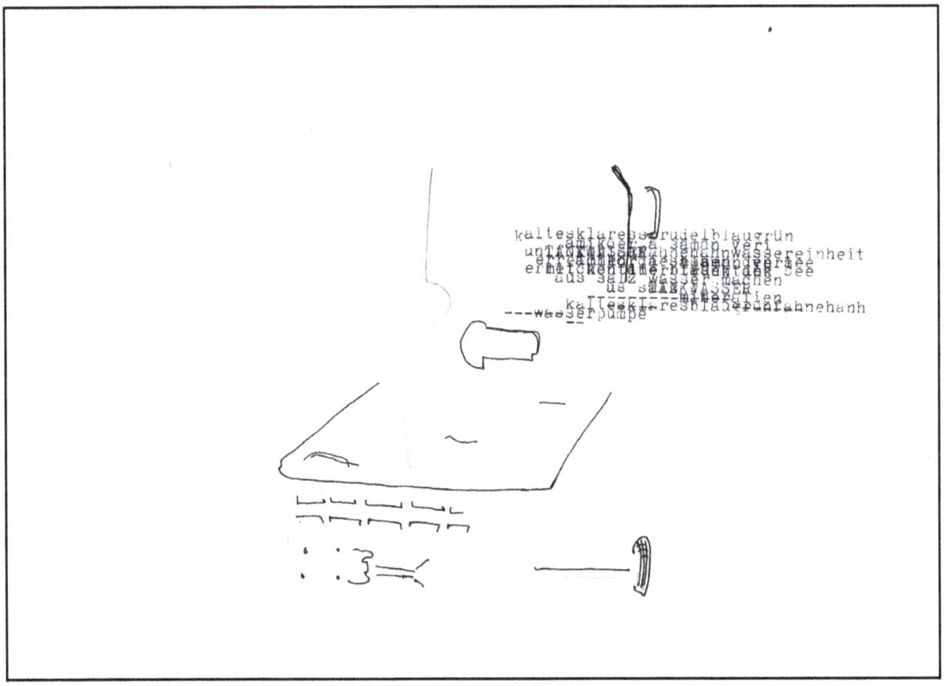
aus salz wasser machen

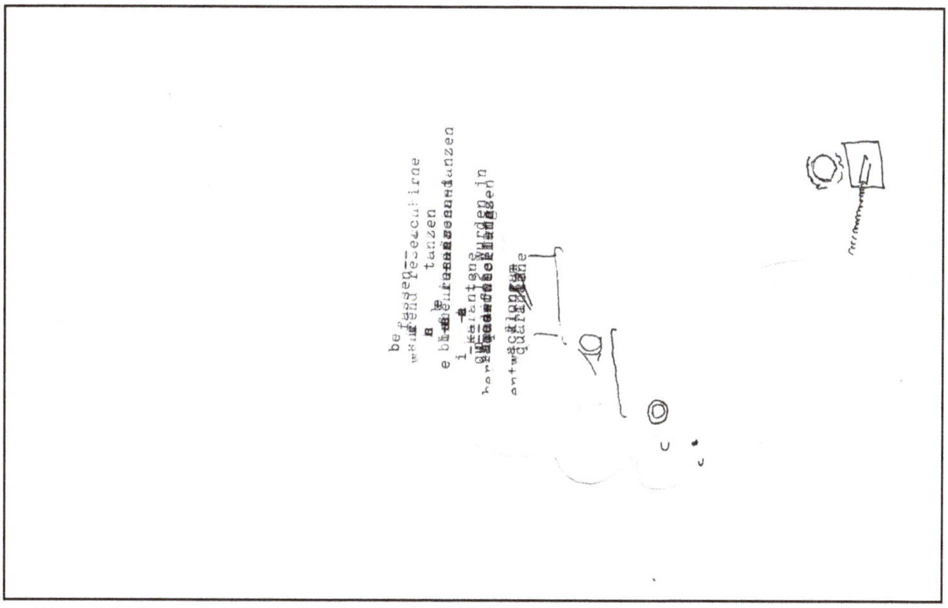

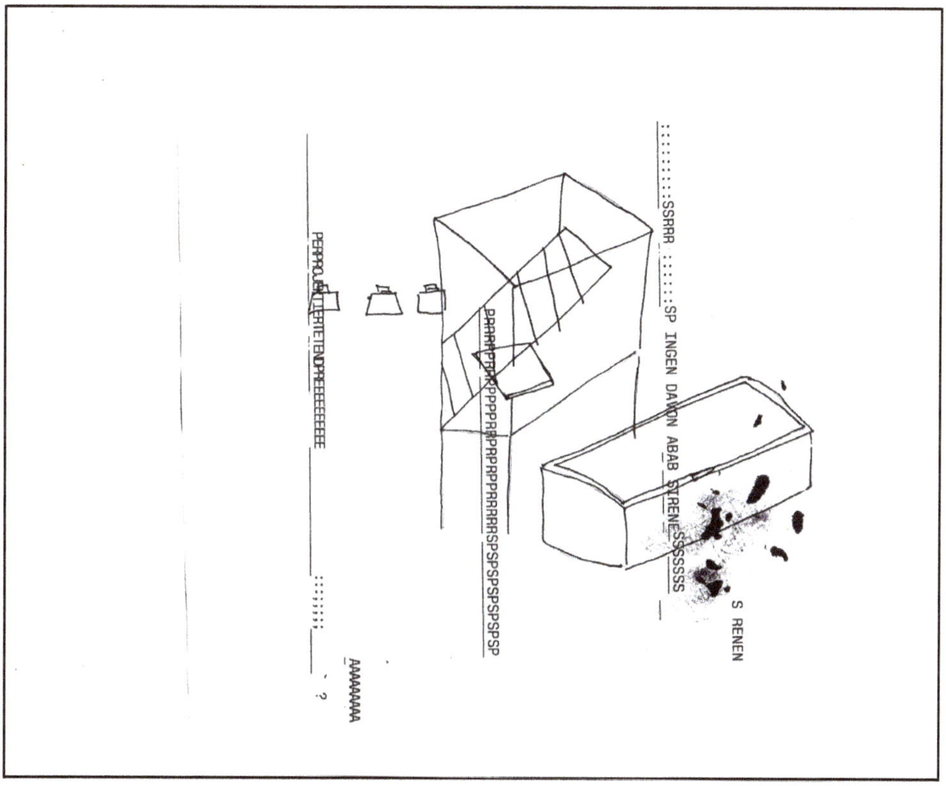

www.ingramcontent.com/pod-product-compliance
Lightning Source LLC
Chambersburg PA
CBHW050257090426
42734CB00023B/3489